fs

Published in 2023 by Latticework Publishing
201-854 Bank Street, Ottawa, K1S 3W3
Designed and typeset by FLOK, Berlin
Printed in the United States by Lightning Source

Men and Rubber: The Story of Business
first published in 1926

Book ISBN: 978-1-7780638-6-2
Ebook ISBN: 978-1-7780638-4-8

Farnam Street Timeless Classics

Men and Rubber:
The Story of Business

—

Harvey S. Firestone

Editor's Note:

This printing of *Men and Rubber: The Story of Business* by Harvey S. Firestone is part of the Farnam Street Timeless Classics Series, where we continue with our goal of 'mastering the best of what other people have figured out.'

This is one of the books I give away the most.

Harvey S. Firestone was one of the leaders of American industry. In a testament to his thoughtful corporate leadership, Firestone tires are still on cars everywhere. Many of the insights he shares on how to start and run a company are as relevant today as when they were originally written.

When I give this book away as a gift, people are always surprised at the number of insights they extract from reading it. The lesson that sticks with people the most is how Firestone's father was properly positioned no matter the circumstances. He was always prepared for the future without predicting it. And that is something we can all do. In fact, one of the most beneficial skills you can learn is how to consistently put yourself in a good position. And this book offers plenty of examples of how to do that.

We have chosen to reprint the book with its original wording. We acknowledge that some passages are problematic. We did, however, feel it would undermine the reprinting to completely remove or edit passages because we don't agree with them.

A secret hiding in plain sight is being able to learn from people with flaws. We hope you can set aside the period of time this was written, and the dated beliefs, and extract the timeless insights you can use. Take the good and reject the rest.

A lot of people republish books like this one that are out of copyright. They clumsily scan a few pages, pop it into a PDF and put it on sale. We took a different approach. Our entire team took a hands-on, detailed, approach on every step, emphasizing quality to make this copy beautiful and timeless.

We know you will enjoy this book and learn from it as much as we have.

Shane and the Farnam Street team

Contents

10 " Good management—that is, management with real thought behind it—does not bother trying to make its way by trickery, for it knows that fundamental honesty is the keystone of the arch of business "

Chapter I
The Labour of Thinking

Thomas A. Edison sums it up this way: "There is no expedient to which a man will not go to avoid the real labour of thinking." He has had it posted on signs about his laboratories; he has said it to me a dozen times and illustrated it with cases. He and Henry Ford often discuss it, and I have often discussed it with Mr. Edison. For the most difficult thing in business is first getting yourself to thinking and then getting others to thinking. I say this is difficult because, in the natural course of business, an infinite number of details come up every day, and it is very easy indeed to keep so busy with these details that no time is left over for hard, quiet thought—for thinking through from the beginning to the end.

An executive cannot grandly dismiss details. Business is made up of details, and I notice that the chief executive who dismisses them is quite as likely as not to dismiss his business. I believe in one-man control—no business is large enough to survive divided authority. Some one man must be supreme, and that man whose authority is supreme, whether or not he be the titular head of the business, has to find the time, not only to know the necessary day-to-day details and progress, but also for quiet, sustained thought.

A man may keep very busy indeed without doing any thinking at all, and the easy course—the course of least resistance—is to keep so busy that there will be no time left over for thought. Almost every man tries to dodge thought or to find a substitute for it. We try to buy thoughts ready-made and guaranteed to fit, in the shape of systems installed by experts. We try to substitute discussion for thought by organizing committees; a committee may function very well indeed as a clearinghouse for thoughts, but more commonly a committee organization is just an elaborate means of fooling oneself into believing that a spell spent in talking is the same as a spell spent in thinking.

Take Mr. Ford. He knows every necessary detail of the far-flung Ford Industries; he always knows what is going on, but he never attends to the execution of details. He does not waste time in dictating and signing notes and letters, or in seeing people whom it is not necessary for him to see; he delegates all this to others. He has assigned no executive duties whatsoever to himself—in fact, he does not even have a desk. He has only a few friends and no social obligations at all, and so he keeps himself free to think and to plan and to watch.

It is commonly imagined that Mr. Ford arrives at his decisions quickly. Nothing could be farther from the fact.

He reaches his decisions slowly and alone; he does not jump at anything, and so, when the time comes for execution, everything moves with marvelous rapidity because everything has been previously thought through and planned. He has had the time to do this thinking and planning because he has used his time himself instead of permitting others to use it for him. And he is certain that plans will be executed for him, because he knows how to let men go when they grow too rich and lazy to execute.

It is really a misnomer to call the directing head of an enterprise an "executive." He cannot possibly be an executive and hold enough time back to think. The execution must be done by others, and one of the vital, ever-present problems, as a company grows wealthy, is keeping executives on the job of executing. Men are apt to swell up and get lazy, and then no price is too high to pay to get rid of them. Mr. Ford manages to keep his people ever quick and active, and in the rare case of a man slowing down in order to get leisure to spend money, Mr. Ford always spots him and gradually relieves him of his more important duties, and finally puts him in a quiet backwater with nothing to do.

Mr. Edison is a profound thinker. His mind is very different from that of Mr. Ford in that, while Mr. Ford thinks both creatively and commercially, Mr. Edison thinks almost wholly creatively and does not give the same order of thought to commerce that he gives to creation. Neither man is an inventor in the ordinary sense, for they do not stumble upon things by accident; they start with what they want to achieve and then think out the methods of achievement.

Mr. Edison is the most widely informed man I have ever come in contact with; not only his scientific knowledge, but also his general knowledge is well-nigh universal. Often, on our camping trips, I have seen him pick up a stick of wood or a stone and talk for an hour on it. One of his favourite amusements is "questions and answers." In this game he is allowed to ask each player a certain number of questions, and each player is allowed to ask him a certain number of questions. When a player fails to answer, he drops out. Mr. Edison always wins, for I have never seen him unable to answer any question put to him, while the questions he puts he usually has to answer himself just to demonstrate that they are answerable!

Mr. Edison's whole life has been devoted to training his mind to concentrated thinking. He will work for hours and days without food or sleep, and he can do this because he has so trained his mind that it shuts out everything excepting the specific problem before him.

Business is founded on thought. Optimism and enthusiasm are valuable in keeping up the morale of an organization—they are lubricants which help to overcome friction—but they cannot be the driving power, and they cannot substitute for well-thought-out business principles, any more than a machine will run just because it is well oiled. Power has to be transmitted before a wheel will turn. We give various names to the thought which has the power to turn the wheels. Sometimes we call it management. But there is another kind of management which is not based on thought and which is not management at all; for instance, there is the kind of management which operates solely on records. Records will guide thought, but they will not substitute for thought. Good management—that is, management with real thought behind it—does not bother trying to make its way by trickery, for it knows that fundamental honesty is the keystone of the arch of business. It knows that you will fail if you think more of matching competitors than of giving service, that you will fail if you put money or profits ahead of work, and that there is no reason why you should succeed if what you do does not benefit others.

This is not idealistic philosophy; it is the hardest kind of hard common sense. If you ask yourself why you are in business and can find no answer other than "I want to make money," you will save money by getting out of business and going to work for someone, for you are in business without sufficient reason. A business which exists without a reason is due for an early death. The single reason for the existence of any business must be that it supplies a human need or want, and, if my experience is worth anything, a business which has this reason for its existence will be bound in the end to prosper if thought be put into it. Thought, not money, is the real business capital, and if you know absolutely that what you are doing is right, then you are bound to accomplish it in due season. I say this not because I read it somewhere in a book, but because I have lived it. For if there is any phase of adversity which our business has not met and beaten, I should like to know it. We chartered the present Firestone Tire & Rubber Company in 1900, making solid tires for carriage wheels. I had a capital of $45,000, which I had earned in a previous carriage-tire company. We had scarcely begun business before we were faced with a great patent suit, second, perhaps, only to the famous Selden patent suit. We had only a little factory with ten men, and I was general manager and sales manager and every other kind of manager. Our capital ran quickly out, and as our business grew, it had to be financed by bank loans and sales of stock. I not only had to sell the tires we made, but also the shares of stock to get the money to make more tires. For years I rarely met a man who seemed to have any money without trying to sell him stock. I sold it to officers of banks with which we did business, I sold it to the people from whom we bought our supplies, I sold it to our own employees, and I bought it myself whenever I could find a bank which would take it as collateral. We financed from hand to mouth, but steadily we grew, and we grew in the face of great tire companies who could have bought us out of their current bank balances.

I sold the stock in the absolute confidence that I was doing a favour to whoever bought it, and in that I was right. For instance, I induced an officer of a steel corporation with which we did business to take, in the first few years, stock to the value of $7,500. For some years he got nothing in return for his money; today his holdings have a market value of $900,000.

We grew from the little building we first bought to larger buildings, and for many years we could not increase our manufacturing capacity in pace with the orders that came in. We fought and won other great patent suits, the loss of any one of which would have wiped us out of existence. Our original ten employees grew to 17,000. We passed from the solid carriage tire to the various forms of automobile tires. Our sales went up to around a hundred million dollars a year, and our capacity from around forty tires a day to around forty thousand. We built up on the side a rim-making business which supplies half the manufacturers of passenger cars and trucks in the country. From only a few scattered salesmen, we grew to sixty-two factory branch houses, seventy-five warehouses, and thirty-six thousand dealers in the United States, and in addition we founded more than a hundred foreign branches and distributors. We applied Mr. Ford's ideas of production and cut out more than half of the hand labour of making tires—which largely increased the average wage of the employees while reducing the price of tires to the consumers. We built a factory in Canada and a rubber mill in Singapore in the Straits Settlements, so that we might save waste in the transport of rubber; we built a thousand homes or more for our employees, and in the year 1919 we earned more than nine million dollars, and our total assets exceeded seventy million dollars, of which nearly one half was surplus. We had four dollars in current assets to every dollar of current liabilities.

We were sailing smoothly with the wind, and we were so strong that we thought nothing could harm us. We had all the bank credit we could possibly use. We dwelt on Easy Street and walked on velvet. Then, in the fall of 1920—not out of a clear sky but out of a sky which looked clear to us, for, in our prosperity, we had stopped thinking through—the tornado swept out, gripped us, and shook us. I was in Europe at the time. Rubber dropped from fifty-five cents to sixteen cents a pound, and with it crashed our tremendous inventories. We owed the banks nearly forty-four million dollars, and some of them wanted their money, and we had no money. I personally owed the banks several million dollars, with Firestone stock as collateral, for whenever I could buy any stock I bought it. I had put everything I earned into this stock, for I believe that a man is not truly in his business unless he has his all in it. The value of this stock had in a few days dropped below the amount of the loans it secured. Both the company's fortune and my personal fortune were hanging out on the end of a limb which threatened at any moment to break. It was a time for quick thinking, but above all for thorough thinking, and in the excitement, everything made for taking action instead of taking thought. But first I took thought, and I took counsel, and then I took action, with the result that we reduced our bank loans twelve million dollars in a couple of months; we ranged up nearly all our banks so that they did everything to help us and nothing to hinder us; we reorganized the inside workings of our company, both in manufacturing and selling; we started to think again, and we carried on through the dullest years the tire industry has ever experienced, to such good purpose that by October 1924, we had paid off every dollar of bank indebtedness and were in far sounder condition than at any previous period. And now, although I date the foundation of the company historically from 1900, I regard those first twenty years only as a period of preparation for the real test of 1920. A business is not a business until it has been hardened by fire and water.

What we lost in the boom—what everyone lost—was the appraisal of values. It does not require any thought to do business in a period of rising prices, and we had gotten out of the way of thinking. Instead of comparing values, the continued rise in prices covered up our mistakes. And it took a great shock to bring us to our senses and make us again appraise values. Much of the thinking in business has to be along the lines of comparing values. If we make a change in manufacturing or in selling methods, will the added return pay the cost? This appraising operation in business is continuous. For instance, in

1920, when we began to compare expenditures and results in our office, we promptly discovered that instead of 1,500 office employees we actually needed only 300—or, in other words, we had 1,200 men performing operations of no value to us. We found an even worse situation in selling; in a period when no selling was necessary since people rushed in to buy, we had built up, because we had lost our sense of values, a most intricate organization that could not possibly pay its way. It was being paid for by rising prices and not by work.

If you employ a man, you appraise his production, and the value of that production to the company is his salary. As his production increases, so should you increase his salary. Keeping this in mind avoids the danger of underpayment or overpayment. One can apply the same rule to personal affairs; what you get out of your automobile in pleasure or in service is the value of the machine to you. If you can get a return of value for the upkeep and inevitable depreciation and that return is above the cost, then you can make money on the car. Otherwise, it will be a loss for you to own it.

17

Many of the values are intangible and cannot be put down on paper in terms of dollars and cents, but this is the point: if you can make a picture of a situation in your own mind, then you can make comparisons and relate values, even if you cannot express them. Some people call this vision, and we hear a deal about the necessity for vision. But vision, as I see it, is not a dreaming forward. It is a thinking through with the values ever in mind. For instance, I should not be exercising vision if I looked forward to a day when I should supply all the tires in the world. That would be just idle, profitless dreaming. In quite another class is thinking out ways and means to get a certain percentage of all the tires used and then relating prices and manufacturing schedules and so on to that end. It is perfectly possible to make an exact mental picture of what would be required to do a decided percentage of business—and if that picture be kept in mind, the decisions to carry it out can come quickly. Quick decisions that have not behind them a long train of thought are exceedingly dangerous. Personally, I do not want to have around me the kind of man who can give me an instant decision on anything I may bring up, for, if he has not had the opportunity to give the question serious thought, then he is only guessing. And I can do my own guessing!

In order to do any good-sized work, one has to build an organization of executives and of employees, and as a business grows, the task is to discover how many of the men will think and how many will just execute orders. There is plenty of room for both kinds of men; the man who only executes is extremely valuable, unless he happens to get into a position where thought is required. The army recognizes this; it not only does not expect the private to think, but actually punishes him for any thought that causes him not to obey orders to the letter—be they right or wrong. Thinking is not required all the way down the line in business. The difficulty is to pick out the men who can and will think and get them into the positions where thought is needed. For instance, a salesman can be a one-act man and still be a success. By "one-act" man, I mean a man who shows a great knowledge of his subject and is really impressive until you happen to get him off his exact line of talk. Then you find that his talk is only an act which he has mastered—that his cleverness is only the repeating of lines which someone else has written. When he has finished his act, he is through. The great trouble with this sort of man is that he may spring his whole act at the wrong time and in the wrong place!

Then one is frequently fooled by the glibness of failures. A man who is a first-class failure—who has had plenty of experience in failing—commonly will talk his head off. He will tell considerably more than he knows, while a thoughtful man will often be none too ready with his answers and usually will tell a little less than he knows. It is the affair of the head of a business to think and to plan broadly and then to select other men who can think and plan within their particular spheres, and finally to select men who can execute. And then, when you have made your selections of men, they are at the best only tentative, for only one out of every hundred men can stand the test of prosperity without losing his sense of values, and fewer still can face adversity without digging in.

This is a queer business of ours. It has changed mightily in twenty-five years. Once upon a time, we sold on mere style. Now we have to sell on service on what we can give a man for his money. And, further, we have to use as our principal raw materials two products which we cannot control and whose prices are continually shifting—that is, rubber and cotton. We have every problem of manufacturing which any business can have; also, we have every problem of selling, for competition is intense; we have seasonal peaks and valleys of demand; we have problems of finance and of forecasting markets, for our production could not, without great waste, meet the peak of demand. We have had one of the biggest booms in history, and also one of the biggest smashes. In short, we have had a little of everything which business can face—and a good deal of some things. But we are here and prospering. It has required some thinking through.

19

20 " No one ever tried to cheat him. This may have been because of respect, or again it may have been because cheating my father required considerably more than the ordinary trader's brains."

Chapter II
Swapping Horses and Ideas

My father, Benjamin Firestone, was, by and large, the best business man I have ever known. The test of a business man is not whether he can make money in one or two boom years, or can make money through the luck of getting into the field first, but whether in a highly competitive field, without having any initial advantage over his competitors, he can outdistance them in a perfect honourable way and keep the respect of himself and of his community.

My father did just that. I have just called him a business man, and that he was, but technically he was a farmer and, as far as I can recall, he never entered into any strictly business enterprise. Our farm at Columbiana, Ohio, which now belongs to me, and where I often take groups of employees on outings, was no better and no worse than the surrounding farms, but year in and year out, my father gained from it upward of two thousand dollars a year in cash—which was a lot of money for a farmer to earn in the 1870s and 1880s out of a couple of hundred acres of land. Sometimes he had especially good seasons when he earned more, but—which is to the point—he never had any really bad seasons, for he seemed always to be able so to balance his affairs that a crop failure which swamped his neighbours did not even touch him.

And I think this was due to the fact that he always had some money on the side and was therefore able to use his best judgment under the circumstances, instead of being forced into a decision by financial pressure.

Having a surplus is the greatest aid to business judgment that I know—and I bitterly know what I am talking about, for I went through years of upbuilding without being able to accumulate a surplus. Then, when I gained one, I saw it completely wiped out and turned into a deficit overnight. A man with a surplus

21

can control circumstances, but a man without a surplus is controlled by them and often he has no opportunity to exercise judgement.

A new business starting without capital or with very little capital cannot, in the very nature of things, at once have a surplus—it must be a fire without a back log to steady its burning. But the first task it ought to set for itself is gaining a surplus. If the business is to be successful, this surplus will have to be accumulated, not out of the moneys which should go for improvement and extension, but out of the profits. A new business which, excepting under the most unusual circumstances, attempts to pay a dividend within the first five years of its existence is courting danger.

My father had the rare foresight to know that a fine crop one year was more or less a fortunate accident and did not set a figure to be followed during future years. Consequently, he always had plenty of money to lend on mortgage to those around him who, although they had all his farming advantages, did not have his foresight.

Most of the farmers round about worked hard—they were the kind that got up before dawn and sat around to start with the first clear light. My father was not this kind of a worker; he was not a hard worker as was commonly known on a farm. My two brothers—Elmer and Robert J.—and I had to work, but we were not driven, and I have no unpleasant memories of grinding away on a farm. Ours was not that sort of a farm. My father seemed to know how to manage and plan so that there were no real rush seasons, excepting, of course, at harvest. And, in consequence, there was probably more work actually done about our farm than on any other thereabouts, for my father farmed thoroughly.

He always fertilized a little more than his fellows; he harrowed just a little better; in every farm operation, he used just a little more care than did the others, and, consequently, his crops were always just a little bit better. The farm was always neat and clean—on rainy days I well remember that we had the steady

22

job of cleaning out around the fences, where on the ordinary farm weeds and rubbish are allowed to collect. His principal money return was from sheep; we kept an average of about four hundred sheep, and every spring he sold off about one hundred and fifty and sheared the rest. He never had to sell his sheep or wool because he was hard up, and hence he always got the top of the market. His reputation for getting a price became so widespread that the wool buyers came to my father first, for they knew that, unless he sold, the other farmers would not sell. If my father did sell, then the buyer's argument with other farmers was simply:

"Ben Firestone sold for forty cents. Isn't that good enough for you?"

He did not believe in trying to run a dairy—he thought that too much work was involved for the results. We kept four or five cows for our own use, and then, each year, he bought and fattened ten or a dozen young steers. And the steers he took to market were always so firm and heavy that he got the top price for them. Of the field crops he sold only wheat; corn and oats he used on the farm. As I grew older, I usually went with him on his trips to buy or sell cattle or sheep, and it was a whole course in trading to watch him at work. First he saw the whole market and heard what everyone had to offer or say—saying almost nothing himself. He often told me:

23

"Never rush in on a deal. Let it come to you."

That is the course he followed, and by the time he was ready to trade, he knew the whole market. If his survey convinced him that the market was not a good one either to buy or to sell in, he simply went home again. He often held his stock a year to get better prices, and he was so good a judge of conditions that I do not recall that he ever made a mistake by holding. If the market were high and seemed to be going higher, he would seldom wait long to sell, and he never held back in the hope that the prices would soar to some impossible figure. Although he probably had never heard of Baron Rothschild's advice never to buy at the top or sell at the bottom, he literally followed it. He never wanted to get more than his stock was worth or to buy stock for less than it was worth, which is probably the reason why everyone in the market respected him and dealt with him fairly.

No one ever tried to cheat him. This may have been because of respect, or again it may have been because cheating my father required considerably more than the ordinary trader's brains. He was far and away the most considerate man I have ever known. I doubt that he had an enemy, and anyone who has ever lent money in a farming section knows how hard it is to lend and collect without making enemies. He was a Christian, worshipping at the Grace Reformed Church, but he was not a fanatic—his disposition was against excessive emotion of any kind. And also, in a day when few farmers read anything, he was a wide reader and accumulated a large fund of knowledge, which is one of the reasons why he was a good farmer. I notice that when all a man's information is confined to the field in which he is working, the work is never as good as it ought to be. A man has to get a perspective, and he can get it from books or from people—preferably from both.

This thing of sleeping and eating with your business can easily be overdone; it is all well enough—usually necessary—in times of trouble, but as a steady diet, it does not make for good business; a man ought now and then to get far enough away to have a look at himself and his affairs. Otherwise, he gets lost in the details and forgets what he is really doing. One often sees that in foremen.

My father came by his distinction naturally enough, for his father, Peter Firestone, was the big man of the neighbourhood and had the biggest house. The first Firestone in America was Nicholas, who was born at Berg und Thal in 1706 and came to the colonies in 1752 with his wife and four sons: John, Matthias, Michael, and Nicholas.

Berg and Thal are two small farming villages situated one mile apart, forty miles northwest of Strasbourg in the Province of Alsace and six miles south of the railroad station of Saar-Union. The villages are very old, no authentic record being extant as to the time of their foundation or incorporation. Berg in 1889 had about one thousand and Thal about eight hundred inhabitants. In early times, these two villages were one, with one charter and one mayor. The combined villages were known as Bergen-thal. Subsequently, two villages were formed with separate and distinct governments. Berg and Thal originally belonged to the German Empire, but were captured by the French in 1681 and were so held until May 10, 1871, when they were recaptured during the Franco-Prussian War by Germans. Now they are again part of France.

We do not know much about the family in the old country prior to 1720 because all the records were destroyed by the burning of the Lutheran Church at Berg. Tradition says that the first Firestones to locate at Berg und Thal were three brothers who came there from the Austrian Tyrol some time in the 15th Century. These brothers were named Nicholas, John, and Theobald.

Theobald married and moved from Berg und Thal to some other country, and nothing further is known of him or his descendants. John and Nicholas raised families and lived and died in Berg und Thal. They were farmers by occupation.

Nicholas settled in Conaco, in what is now Franklin County, Pennsylvania. His son Nicholas took a farm at Natural Bridge, Rockbridge County, Virginia. He had five daughters and three sons. One of these sons, also named Nicholas, worked out to Columbiana County, Ohio, where he died in 1847. He had four daughters and four sons, and it was his son Peter who was my grandfather. I never knew him, but from all accounts he was an upstanding man, fully ready to make his way on the frontiers. He got a grant of six hundred and forty acres from the government, cleared and planted it, and in a little while was the richest man in the section. I do not know how much actual money he had, but it did not require much money to be rich in those days. At any rate, he was rich enough to feel the necessity of building a great house.

Why is it that a man, just as soon as he gets enough money, builds a house much bigger than he needs? I built a house at

Akron many times larger than I have the least use for; I have another house at Miami Beach which is also much larger than I need. I suppose that before I die I shall buy or build other houses which also will be larger than I need. I do not know why I do it—the houses are only a burden. But I have done it, and all my friends who have acquired wealth have big houses. Even so unostentatious a man as Henry Ford has a much bigger house at Dearborn than he really cares about. I wonder why it is. Perhaps it is some foolish survival of the ancient feudal idea when a big house meant a strong house in which one might keep a small army for protection. In a few cases, a big house is built just as an advertisement that one is rich; sometimes a big house is built so that great entertainments may be given. But in most cases, and especially with men who have earned their own money, the house is just built, and when it is done, no one quite knows why it was ever started. No end of men build their houses so large that they might as well live in a hotel, and then many of them do live in a public hotel rather than go to the bother of running a private hotel.

Anyhow, the spirit was strong in Grandfather Peter, who, otherwise a sensible man, set his people to making bricks and out of them constructed a house much larger than he or any of his descendants have been able to use. And I have not the least doubt that, if anyone asked him why he built it, he would not have known!

When he died, he divided the farm among the sons with the provision that his wife, my grandmother, should live in the big house and choose which of the sons was to maintain it. She chose my father, and she always had two rooms in the house to occupy whenever she saw fit. She lived with us much of the time, but also she visited about among the other brothers, for we now had a considerable community of Firestones.

My father married Catherine Flickinger in 1863, when he was thirty-two years old—there had been some notion that he would be a bachelor, for people married early in those days—and on December 20, 1868, I was born in the old brick house.

My mother—and she died in 1916—had an ability which matched my father's, but it was a different kind of ability. She was not only lovable and kind and intelligent, but also she was a diplomat, and sometimes I suspect she managed my father. At least, I know there never seemed to be any differences in the family, and things moved along very smoothly. From the time we got on our feet in the rubber business up until her death, she every year had down on the farm all of the superintendents, foremen, department heads, and others of the company. Our old house was almost one of the company's buildings, and my mother was so often at Akron meeting the people of the company and of the town that she was a kind of unofficial executive. She really would have been a splendid head for the human side of the company—which is the most important—for she knew people and how to get on with them.

Although I did not dislike farm work, it was the buying and selling of stock, and especially of horses, that most attracted me, and by the time I was fifteen, I could hold my own with anyone in a horse trade. For, first of all, I knew horses and loved them, and then my father trained me, as I have said, never to rush in on a deal. I cannot give any principles for horse trading; it is an art, not a science, and it has to start with liking to be with horses and to know them. Ever since I was a boy, no matter how hard up I might happen to be, I seldom was without at least one horse, and that was always a good one.

It took quite a while to convince my father that I knew anything about horses, but eventually he did defer to my judgment in everything that had to do with horses, while he attended to the cattle, for he knew cattle. It seemed to me, comparing the results of these trading operations with the results from farming, that business offered more opportunities than the farm. Both my father and mother, if they did not encourage me in this view, at least did nothing to discourage me, for they had enough money not to be forced to keep me on the farm as an asset. One of the tragedies of farm life is forcing the children to stay on the farm just to get the work through. We were fortunate in having a first-class high school at Columbiana, and after I graduated from that, I spent three months at the Spencerian Business College in Cleveland, getting ready to enter business.

Our family business ideal of the time was my father's first cousin, Clinton D. Firestone, the principal owner of the Columbus Buggy Company, which was then the most important in the United States, turning out those fine-looking, expensive buggies which years ago it was the ambition of every farmer to own. My older brother, Elmer, was already working in the company, and I wanted very much to get there, but Cousin Clinton did not have a place for me at the moment, and wrote to me at Cleveland that he had found a position for me keeping books in the coal business of John W. Taft in Columbus—a distant relation of President Taft. As a special favour, I suppose, I was paid thirty dollars a month instead of the usual bookkeeper's pay of from fifty to seventy-five dollars a month.

It was thought good business in those days to pay a man as little as he would take, and certainly thirty dollars a month was little enough. We operated as the Royal Coal & Mining Company and sold coal at wholesale, just as did so many other little coal concerns in Ohio at the time. I started work in January and managed to get out of my occupation a most complete and thorough detestation of bookkeeping in all its forms. I wanted to buy and sell things, not just to post the results of transactions—and, anyway, there is not enough real buying and selling in coal to keep a salesman's wits working. In addition to Mr. Taft, we had in the office O. D. Jackson, a middle-aged man, who occupied what we should today call desk room. As a young man he had gone into the Hocking Valley, established a store, made money, bought coal lands with his profits, and made more money. Then he moved from Jacksonville to Columbus to live on the royalty from his mines. We became good friends, and he paid me ten dollars a month to keep his books—which helped a lot, for on thirty dollars a month I had not been able to save anything and could not follow my father's principle of always having something on the side. I managed to save that extra ten dollars a month.

Mr. Taft's business did not amount to very much at the best, and when in the fall of the year he fell ill, he closed it out, and, of course, with it went my job. Clinton Firestone was by that time ready for me, but Jackson and I had been talking over other plans, by which we both expected to make a great deal of money. I went to my cousin Clinton, painted the plans grandly to him, and told him I could not take his job. He did not like it at all—rich relations do not like to have poor relations turn down their offers; we were not poor by any means, but we were poor as compared with Cousin Clinton. He said very brusquely:

"All right, young man, do just as you like. I'll give you three months to be around here again begging me for a job."

That speech hurt me a good deal, but I had the sense to be quiet and not to say what was on my lips, that I would never take a job from him. For, as it later turned out, he was right and I was wrong, and I did take a job from him.

Jackson was a friend of August Green, a worthy widely known as the proprietor of "Green's August Flower," which was a concoction guaranteed to cure anything. You could take it inwardly, or you could take it outwardly; you could cure your children with it, or you could cure the horses, the cattle, and the chickens. August was not what might be called modest in his advertisements, and it appeared that a family which kept a bottle of the "Flower" always in the house might scoff at illness in man or beast. The stuff was quite harmless; it could not retard any one's recovery and, being very pleasant to take, it made Green wealthy. Jackson, having plenty of spare time, had analyzed Green's success and put it down to advertising. He thought that by personal salesmanship without advertising he could duplicate Green's success at a smaller sales cost—wherein he made his mistake.

He had about fifty thousand dollars in cash, in addition to his income from royalties, and with this we planned an organization to be known as the Jackson Manufacturing Company, making a number of products so as to cover the ground much more completely than did Green with his single product. He hired a chemist who developed Jackson's Flavouring Extracts, which we intended to sell to druggists and grocers, just so that the salesmen could present a full line, but our big money was to be made out of a tonic, a cough syrup, a liniment, and an

29

"Arabian Oil," which was a horse liniment. He hired about a dozen salesmen—all of them crack salesmen, according to the then standards of what was a crack salesman. I remember one man in particular to whom he paid the enormous salary of two hundred and twenty-five dollars a month; his name was Wetzel—a big, fine fellow, with a genial presence and the gift of gab. Wetzel was one of those men who could "sell anything." He had just one formula: he just breezed in on a prospect, offered him a cigar, and then sat down and talked him to death. That was salesmanship in those days.

To me Jackson offered fifty dollars a month and expenses—not because I was a salesman, but because I had been with him in working out the plans. That was not only big money, but it opened the way to travel and, like every youngster, I wanted to see the world and more especially to see it grandly, as I imagined travelling salesmen saw it. No wonder I turned down my cousin's offer to take a place behind a desk in a buggy factory!

The first town I made was Applecreek, Ohio. I had thought that I was going to make my impress on the whole country, but I found that Jackson had assigned me to the little Ohio towns where the star salesmen would not bother to go. But anyway, I was a salesman, and I very proudly swung off the train at Applecreek and tried to register at the little hotel with exactly the manner I thought a trained salesman ought to have. I strutted all I could before the hangers-on, encircling the stove on tilted chairs. Then I went out to sell and my courage quit.

I surveyed the town. It had two large general stores, one on each side of the railroad track, and several small stores. I walked around the town two or three times, wondering what I would say if I did go into a store to sell. Finally I kicked some nerve into myself and tried the smallest store in the town. I do not remember what I said, but it could not have been very important, because I did not even come near to making a sale. Then I tried two more of the smaller stores and still no sales. Then I made for the biggest store and offered my flavouring extracts, keeping the patent medicines in the background. I made a sale—and also I discovered something.

The proprietors of the little stores would not bother to listen to me. Although they did not seem to be doing anything, they said they were too busy to talk with me. The proprietor of the big store was busy—but he had plenty of time to listen to my story and to find out if he could make money out of what I had to sell. From that time onward, I have never found it worthwhile to bother with thoroughly little fellows for, realizing their weakness, they are always on the defensive, while a larger man will listen to what you have to say and be quick to grasp any money-making opportunities you may have to offer. By a "big man" I do not mean the man who has a big business—he may be just on his way to having a big business. But unless a man on the first approach shows signs of wanting to make money, it is a waste of time to try to convince him that he ought to buy. You may, if you persist, eventually sell to the suspicious man, but I have not found that it pays to make the effort—the returns are not commensurate with the work involved. Thereafter, when I entered a town, I always tried the largest and not the smallest store first.

In the meantime, the crack salesmen would not bother with the small sales of flavouring extracts, they went out after the big money of the patent medicine and they did not sell. Patent medicines do not sell on merit, for there is precious little merit in most of them. Patent medicines sell only on their reputation for curing diseases, and that reputation has to be built up by advertising—people have to be made to believe that the medicines do good. That is where Jackson fell down. He had not built up any belief in his medicines through advertising.

My little sales of flavouring extracts were the largest income the company had. The extracts did not need to be advertised, because people did not have to be educated into the belief that vanilla extract will give a vanilla flavour, whereas they do have to be educated or fooled into the belief that a spring tonic will cure spring ills. Within six months all the star salesmen had quit, and Jackson was broke—and I was out on the road.

" Salesmanship has to establish a continuing relation in which the seller helps the buyer."

Chapter III
Wild Rose Lotion

My two big lines working for Jackson were vanilla extract, which I sold for twelve dollars a gallon and which cost four dollars a gallon to produce, and "Wild Rose Lotion" for chapped hands, which I sold at a dollar and a half a dozen bottles and which cost fifty cents a dozen. I did not have any luck with the patent medicines, for I could never make a convincing demonstration, for the reason (although I did not recognize it at the time) that there was nothing in the patent medicines to demonstrate. And I could not get any conviction into my story of what they were supposed to do. The extracts and the lotion were actually good, and I believed in them and stood ready to back them against anything of the kind offered.

Thereby, quite unconsciously, I turned up the first principle of salesmanship—which is that you must thoroughly believe in what you have to sell. Then selling becomes merely a matter of showing how your product will help a prospect. I have always been more of a salesman than a manufacturer—it has been hard for me to learn factory methods. But selling has always come easy to me, simply because, since those patent medicines, I have never attempted to sell anything which I did not thoroughly believe in. Therefore, I have never really had to sell at all—only to explain the favour I expected to do the prospect. The principle holds true, whether one is selling a tangible thing, like a rubber tire, or whether one is selling something intangible, like the future of the company, either in the shape of capital stock or in the shape of credit at a bank. Persuading a man to buy is not, to my notion, salesmanship. It is just persuading him to buy and nothing more.

Salesmanship has to establish a continuing relation in which the seller helps the buyer. Going to great lengths to sell a man something he does not want is a clumsy way of trying to get money—it is much simpler and just as honest to knock the fellow on the head and take the money away from him.

Jackson, as I said, went broke, and the star salesmen, having regularly drawn their salaries until there was nothing more to draw from, promptly sought new pastures. I was the only salesman who lasted out the year, and that was because I did not know any better. It was hard going. Jackson tried premiums; he gave nutcrackers and nutpicks and odds and ends of plated silver to purchasers of beyond a certain quantity of the patent medicines. This was bad business. The kind of merchant who will buy goods for resale, not on the goods themselves but on some foolish present that you offer him in addition, is not the kind of merchant who can ever do enough business to become a profitable customer. Jackson tried every scheme he knew of, except advertising, and when he eventually got around to the point where he knew he ought to advertise, he did not have the money. He had spent it all in paying the salaries and living expenses of star salesmen.

I have never hired star salesmen and I never will. They are just an expense. It is the duty of management to provide so good a product and then to let people know so thoroughly about it that any man of reasonable intelligence can go out and sell it. If there is no real salesmanship in the home office, there most certainly will be none on the road. Jackson kept me out because I earned money for him. Not a week passed in which I did not earn my keep, selling small lots to grocery stores, ice cream parlours, and drug stores. But it began to be harder and harder to stay on the road, for Jackson had trouble in scraping together enough money to pay me and my expenses, for out of the orders I turned in, he had both to supply the goods and support himself, so often there was nothing left over for me. The final week came at Crestline, Ohio, about a hundred miles from Columbus. Neither my expense check nor my salary check came in on Monday as they should have. This did not bother me, because the check seldom arrived on time, but when Tuesday came without a check, I began to get worried, for I was due to move on and also I had spent all the money I had with me. I was afraid to telegraph Jackson, because Crestline was a small town and the news that I had no money might get around, so I just waited. Wednesday came without a check, and I began to worry about being put out of the hotel.

I had already covered the town, and there was not a thing for me to do. It struck me that if the hotel people saw me just sitting around, they would ask me for money. So every day, bright and early, I started out with my grip as though I were working; I walked the streets until dinner, then started out again in the afternoon and walked until supper. On Saturday my money came, and with it I got back to Columbus. Jackson had sent to me—he was fair—his last money, and he had quit. And once more I was without a job.

My cousin Clinton soon heard the bad news and offered me another job—being considerate enough not to take advantage of the opportunity to rub his previous advice in on me. For nine months I worked in the shipping room; then he promoted me to salesman in the Columbus showroom, where I learned how to sell buggies. Our Des Moines branch got into considerable trouble, and my cousin, remembering that I was a bookkeeper, sent me out to put it straight. I stayed there for some months until things were in working order, when I was shifted to the Detroit agency as a bookkeeper. I had by then developed no greater liking for keeping books than when I was in the coal office, and I managed to edge into the showroom during my spare time and help sell. As a result, I got entirely into the sales end and was given the district outside of Detroit.

Then I began to come into my own and make some money. Almost immediately I started in to accumulate horses. With most people, keeping horses is an expense, but I found I could buy and sell horses so as not only to cover all the expense of keeping them, but also to have a profit. I lived pretty high in those days, keeping up with people who could afford to own horses for the fun of it, while I had to make them pay their own way. I was earning $150 a month, and I usually kept one or two first-class horses, a light buggy and a little racing sulky, for, in the late afternoons and on Saturday afternoons, we liked to have our brushes on the Boulevard, and I usually managed to have at least one horse, which, while it might not be the best on the road, was never the worst.

Sometimes I drove horses for other men. My greatest triumph

was with a big, wild sort of horse that had great speed but simply would not race. Either he would not start, or somewhere in the race he would go wild and cut up. I thought he was not being handled rightly, and the owner gave him to me to race. The whole thing was to get that horse's confidence, and after weeks of effort I got it; he came to believe that nothing could happen to him if I were driving. I tried him out behind a buggy on the Boulevard, and he was able to pass anything. Then I entered him in a gentlemen's race on a private mile track near Detroit.

The entry was taken as a joke, and I made no pretence it was other than a joke, for I was afraid he would get cold feet in the race—as he always did. Still, I took the chance. There were four or five horses in the race, and in the first heat I kept my horse back, just letting him trail along and giving him no chance at all to get nervous. I used that heat merely as a practice spin to show him that he really had nothing to fear. In the second heat, having more confidence, he started without difficulty, but I kept him in until the stretch; then I let him go and he won. The crowd was all up for the third heat—it was two out of three—every man in the race was wealthy except me, and the crowd was rooting for me. Going to the start was the biggest thrill I ever had. I had wanted to trail in that heat and then go ahead on the stretch, but I had the pole position, and if I let the bunch get far ahead, I would have to go completely around them in the stretch. On the other hand, I was afraid that if my horse cut ahead too soon he would think there was nothing more to work for and decide to stop running. I compromised by holding him back just enough to prevent the next horse from taking the pole away from us and as we came into the stretch I let him go for all he was worth. And go he did! He went so fast and so true that we won that race by at least three or four lengths.

In this, my first prosperity, I met Miss Idabelle Smith, the daughter of Mr. and Mrs. George T. Smith of Jackson, Michigan. George T. Smith was the inventor of the process that turns out the present-day "patent" and "half-patent" flour, by which is removed those elements which gave a dark colour to the bread and cake made from the old millstone flour. On November 20, 1895, we were married—I being then twenty-seven years old and rated as a successful business man.

But this prosperity was not long to continue; our company sold a very fine buggy which cost one hundred and ten dollars, while Durant, Dort, Nash, and some others whose names afterward also became famous in the automobile field, were bringing out good, strong buggies to sell at thirty-five dollars. For a while, the farmers who could afford it bought our more expensive buggy as a matter of pride, but they soon began to find out that they were throwing their money away and that it was cheaper to buy the less expensive buggy and get a new one every few years rather than hang on to our old, expensive affair. Our business gradually fell off throughout the country, although I did a fair business in Michigan, and just a few months after I was married our company failed, leaving me once more without a job—but this time with the responsibility of a wife and a home.

I did some selling for the receiver of the company during the next several months, but this was not enough to keep me going, and I kept my eyes open for other work.

Driving out one afternoon in my rubber-tired buggy, it for the first time struck me that my future was right on the wheels of my buggy. Those rubber tires were the only ones in Detroit. They were not the only ones in the United States, and a London cab company had already fitted out all its cabs with rubber tires. But they were hard to buy in the United States. Why not make them easy to buy? I had about a thousand dollars saved, which was not enough to start business on. I knew that. I cast about among my friends and selected a man who I thought would make a good partner and who had money. Then I invited him for a drive; and I took some pains to let him realize how much easier the riding was than with steel-rimmed wheels. Actually, I was making a demonstration, but without any proposition; I wanted him to sell himself before I did any talking. We had dinner together, and I told him what I had in mind—that if he and I both thought that rubber tires were a great improvement over steel, others could be made to think likewise, and we had before us a new business that might grow to any extent. Of course, I figured out the number of buggies in the United States, and then said that if we sold only one half of those owners, we could have a business like Standard Oil. At length he agreed with me and said he would go into the business. He was from Chicago and recalled an old, run-down rubber factory there on Wabash Avenue near Harrison Street, which he thought could be bought cheaply. That very night we took the train for Chicago and within a couple of days had taken over the factory for fifteen hundred dollars cash. The machinery in it did not amount to anything, but we did not need much machinery, for we intended to buy our tires in strips that looked a deal like garden hose, except that they were solid, and then simply cut the strips to buggy-wheel size and cement the ends together. The tires of those days slipped on like baby-carriage tires, and one workman and I were at first enough to attend to all the business. When I sold a set of tires, I took the buggy wheels back to the shop, and the workman and I cut the rubber tire to size and cemented it on the wheel over the steel rim. We got about forty dollars for a set of tires, which cost us about fourteen dollars. We paid forty dollars a month rent for the shop, and I paid twenty-five dollars a month for a little house—our grocery bill hardly averaged five dollars a week. Sometimes it seems that it might be better to go back to those simpler days, that one might get more out of a less complex life. But it cannot be done. One changes with prosperity. We all think we should like to lead the simple life, and then we find that we have picked up a thousand little habits which we are quite unconscious of because they are a part of our very being—and these habits are not in the simple life. There is no going back—except as a broken man.

Our cash capital was around five hundred dollars. With that we organized the Firestone-Victor Rubber Company, which later became the Firestone Rubber Tire Co. From the very beginning we prospered; once a man rode on rubber tires, he wanted a set. Although we did not sell many nationally, we did sell in Chicago. But we had not enough money to expand and to swing our stocks. We bought our rubber at first from the Morgan &

Wright Company at Chicago and later from the India Rubber and Diamond Rubber companies at Akron. These big rubber companies were better equipped to do a carriage-tire business than we were, but they did not seem quite to understand tires, and then, too, the volume of the business was small—it was just a specialty.

All of the active management was in my hands. The production end did not give much trouble, for it was simple enough, but the finances far from simple. Their complexity was not due to the size of the operations—I could state our condition in those days right out of my head, and the back of an envelope gave ample space for the statement. Our trouble was that we did not have enough money and did not know how to get it. I did sell the Morgan & Wright Company on giving us a credit of $1,000, but I did not know anything about getting a line of credit at a bank. The only way open—or so it seemed to me—was to get more money invested, and it is not easy to persuade people to put money into a new enterprise. However, I did persuade one of my friends to come with us for a small amount. And that helped for a while. But we were growing faster than our capital, which meant that we were always short of money.

Near our little plant was the more modern plant of the Imperial Rubber Company, and one day its proprietor offered to sell out to me lock, stock, and barrel for $15,000. He had not been able to make money against the competition of the big rubber companies. We did not have that much money, but the plant seemed to be a good buy, and I set out to raise the money; and for the first time I entered a bank with the intention of borrowing money. I shall not mention the name of the bank, for we never afterward did business with it. I talked with the president for a few moments, and then he turned me over to the credit man. I had with me a statement from our books, which I had prepared myself, because, as a bookkeeper, I was used to making up statements and I kept the books of the concern. The credit man read the statement carefully; I have forgotten what sort of a statement it was, but since it was a true statement, it probably showed our liquid assets as small—less than our current liabilities. For almost everything we had was tied up in

39

plant, equipment, and raw materials. I did not at the time know that bank loans were made on the basis of quick assets and that banks do not commonly care to go into the investment business. If we had assets and prospects, it did not bother me at all what form they were in. The credit man led me on to explain the statement and I thought that I was selling our future. I told the story of the business we were doing, and how much we needed money to expand and take over the new plant, and what we expected to do with the money.

He seemed to grow more interested as I proceeded, and I thought to myself that, when I had finished, he would recommend giving me the bank. But he was just giving me the opportunity to show how little I knew about finance. He was not frank about it—I left that bank thinking I was going to get a loan. And, while I was never refused the loan, I never got it. However, I did learn something.

What I learned was that a bank statement ought never to be in such shape that it has to be explained. Everything ought to be on the statement, and if for some reason an explanation of an item is asked for, then one should be able to present facts and not prospects. A statement of condition can be a prospectus—in fact, it is the best possible kind of prospectus—but it ought not to be prepared in enthusiasm. It ought to be absolutely frank and entirely conservative; then an explanation will show that actual conditions are a little better and not a little worse than represented. A young fellow gets anxious, and he will, with perfect sincerity, paint far too rosy a picture. I do not blame that bank man for turning me down, but I do blame him for leading me on. Thinking the incident over, I saw that I had rushed in instead of going in cautiously and with a full knowledge of facts.

Another mistake I had made was in trying to borrow money from a bank without vision instead of from a bank with vision—although I had found out in selling that it did not pay to deal with small people. In a day or two, I had my new plans all worked out, and I went to a big bank—to the First National—and was turned over to a young officer, whose manner attracted me extraordinarily, for he seemed to sympathize with me and want to help me. And goodness knows, I needed both help and sympathy, for, while I was willing to take a shy at being a financier, my partners would not go even that far. If any money were to be raised, I had to raise it. This young man went into my statement, he asked me direct questions about my business, and I answered them frankly and honestly. I did not make the mistake of overselling him. Incidentally, we did not have an account in that bank, and I had just come in off the street without an introduction of any sort. But this bank officer did not bring up opening an account; he showed me where I had made mistakes in financial management. He told me something about how I should try to keep a ratio between quick assets and liabilities, and in an hour, not only found out all about what we were doing, but also gave me a course in practical banking. Then he lent me $10,000 on the company note.

The young man's name was Frank O. Wetmore, and today he is the president of the bank and one of the best friends our company has. He gave me my first lessons in banking, and while we did business in Chicago, I never made a move without first talking it over with him. Today I never go to Chicago without going in to see him, for he is as much of an advisor now as he was then. And I may say that, very shortly, we opened an account with the First National and have been doing business with it ever since. If you want help, it pays to go where the brains are.

I had no idea that bank money cannot safely be used for capital investments. It is entirely true that it ought not to be, but the man who can build a business on small capital and preserve fine distinctions as to the use of the money he borrows is yet to be born. And every banker of experience knows it!

We bought the new factory largely with the bank money and some additional money we raised. Our assets had risen to a total of $40,000, on a most conservative basis, but also we had plenty of liabilities. The Rubber Tire Wheel Company appeared in the market with a wheel especially made for taking rubber tires, which was much superior to our crude method.

They threatened to drive us out of business, so I decided to persuade them to consolidate with us, even though they had assets of around two hundred thousand dollars. It was not hard to show that, if the two of us kept in the field, neither would make money, and in due course we consolidated. The result made us the biggest factor in the buggy tire business. In fact, I once placed an order in Akron for half a million dollars' worth of tires.

The Consolidated Company, forming as a trust to take over all the rubber companies of the country, made an offer to buy us out. We made no haste to accept; we traded back and forth a little, and finally sold out for $1,254,000—or something more than four times what our business was worth, not counting its goodwill. Out of the payments I received $45,000 in cash, which was considerably more money than I had thought was in the world for me. Of this sum I invested $20,000 in a 6 percent mortgage, so that I might have a steady income to fall back on. The other $25,000 I kept in the bank in cash ready to see what might turn up. We had been in business only about four years, and my original $1,000 had grown to $45,000. I took a position with the new company, but I did not hold it for long, because I wanted to be out for myself. I resigned to look about to see what I could do with my new money.

44 "A business which starts off quickly, makes money at once, and seems to be in every respect a gold mine, often does not last long. It is just selling peanuts to the crowd in town for the circus—a once-around affair."

Chapter IV

Starting the Company

Having some money in hand, I wanted to go into business for myself. If a man has no capital, it is usually a waste of time for him to start in business on his own, unless he can borrow capital for a long term at low interest. But the chances of success on borrowed capital are slight. It is not possible in beginning a new enterprise to see ahead far enough to discover how much capital really will be needed.

It is unusual, and indeed abnormal, for a concern to make money during the first several years of its existence. The initial product and the initial organization are never right. The first product, no matter how thoroughly it has been thought out, has to be seasoned in the market. An experienced company with ample resources can make extensive laboratory tests, and also tests in use, for a long period before bringing out a product, and can reduce many of the elements of luck and risk. But it cannot know in advance either how the public will receive that product or how it will stand up in actual service. The new company will think that it has taken every precaution. It will think that it has made every sort of an investigation, but really the most searching trials that a new company can make are of small moment, first, because the promoters can never get themselves into the cold, detached frame of mind in which the public approaches anything new, and, second, because the knowledge of what really is a test will be lacking.

The business of any live company has to be constantly revised, but with a new company these revisions have to be drastic. In the exceptional case where the product itself does not have to be revamped, its method of manufacture will have to be changed, and if neither the product nor its manufacture has to be changed, then, most certainly, the human organization—be it three men or a thousand—will prove inadequate.

It is difficult enough to pick men in a seasoned business, but then one has at least the advantage of knowing something about the required duties. In starting a new business, although a paper organization may be put down in a small way, the eventual organization will turn out to be something very different. It is always cut and try in business, but in the beginning this cutting and trying have to go on so rapidly that there is not much chance really to make money. It may be possible in exceptional cases to pay the interest on borrowed capital, but unless one strikes a bonanza, any undertaking quickly to pay back borrowed capital is bound to result in failure. It is more than unsafe—it is just a waste of time—to start into business with money that has not been embarked for better or for worse—that is, money which demands no return other than the profits the business can afford—which means money invested in stock and in common stock rather than preferred.

Also, it is exceedingly unwise to hold out any promises of quick returns—although it is human nature to do so. For if a new business does succeed, it will have to be uncommonly careful in the distribution of profits. If you are going ahead, you will need every cent you can lay your hands on to finance operations, and the more of these operations you can finance with your own money, the better off you are. A business which starts off quickly, makes money at once, and seems to be in every respect a gold mine, often does not last long. It is just selling peanuts to the crowd in town for the circus—a once-around affair.

I thought I had money enough to go into business. I had $45,000, and I was strongly advised that it was too much money to hazard in business—that it was a fortune to retire on! At that time it was the desire of every ambitious young man to have his own business. The great corporation had not yet gotten under way, with the exception of the Standard Oil Company, which was thought of more as a mysterious phenomenon than as a type for future business. Today it hardly pays a young man to go into business for himself, unless he has a new idea which he cannot sell to any one. The rewards of big business today are greater than the individual can hope to achieve alone. Ability is rewarded more highly than it used to be—not because men are more generous than formerly, but because a big concern has to have big management, and big management costs money.

In my early days, the head of the concern usually owned most of it and he considered his employees more as servants than as colleagues. Good management is no less personal than ever it was, but in a business of any size a certain amount of judgment and executive duty simply must be delegated, and unless the delegates have pay commensurate with their abilities and responsibilities, they are bound to become time-servers, and the business will go to ruin.

The best course today is to go into the organization which has already accumulated capital and get a wide scope for one's ability. But there is no rule. While this is being written, probably some man with only a few dollars in his pocket is founding a business that will, within the next twenty years, run into the millions. Since I have started in business, I have seen the motion pictures and the radio grow into vast industries in the hands of men who only here and there had any capital to start with.

47

I had the capital but I did not have an idea. I knew the carriage business, and I knew the carriage-tire business. I had no hankering after the carriage business, for it had become one of keen competition in cheap models. That had wrecked my uncle's buggy business. The gasoline automobile was not then a factor and gave no promise of being what it is today. The few cars on the road were mostly of foreign make and owned by rich men, and, although not exactly toys, they were certainly not commercial products. But I did believe in the electrically driven vehicle. I had sold many tires to the Woods Motor Vehicle Company in Chicago, which was one of the first companies to get out an electric carriage. The storage batteries in these early cars were cumbersome, but it seemed only a question of time until the weight of the batteries would be reduced and their life lengthened. We all thought of electricity as the coming motive power for everything. The few domestic gasoline cars which I had seen impressed me as being ingenious rather than useful. I do not recall ever having seen Henry Ford's car about the streets of Detroit, and I have no recollection of having seen Mr. Ford, although probably we passed many times on the street, for the Detroit Edison Company where he worked was close by my old Detroit office. I believed thoroughly in rubber tires. They made riding so much easier that they appeared to me to be a necessity. The tires had not been developed to a point where they could economically be used on the heavier delivery wagons and trucks, but that development was only a question of time. I am speaking of solid and cushion tires, for at that time I did not see any advantage in pneumatics and I did see a great many disadvantages in them. Time has proved that I was right about rubber tires in general, for there is hardly a motor-drawn vehicle in the world without them. I have revised my opinion about pneumatics, but I still retain a strong liking for cushion tires—which is probably the reason why our present company makes so many of them for heavy duty.

Before I really had a chance to make up my mind about the future, the Kelly-Springfield Tire Company offered me the position of manager in Chicago, and I took it. The sales policy of the company did not prove to my liking. The practice was to charge tires at the cost of material and labour and on top of that a royalty. This seemed to me essentially unsound; the seller ought to make an inclusive price and have done with it. In about eight months I took a vacation, and in Cleveland made up my mind to get out and sent in my resignation. Then I set about the organization of a tire company of my own. I had no difficulty in raising the money and the company would have gone through, but the bankers, who were helping in the promotion, had on their hands a piece of property which they were extremely anxious to get rid of. They insisted that we take it as a factory—in spite of the fact that it was in no way suited for tire making. If the organizers of a corporation cannot agree at the beginning, there is small chance that they will afterward, so I simply dropped the negotiations. A company in Akron manufacturing twist drills and forgings also had a tire department but not a satisfactory tire, so they took license on a tire I had developed and patented and asked me to be its manager. I accepted, but once more the policy did not suit me; this time, instead of resigning, I took an option to buy the department. Akron was the home of the rubber tire industry. It was a good town for any man interested in tire making, for the big Goodrich, Goodyear, and Diamond factories were there, and also plenty of workmen who knew tires. The tire trade was largely in solid tires and in the single-tube pneumatics used on bicycles. Pneumatic tires were not popular for carriages; they gave easier riding, it is true, but under the extra weight of a carriage their single tubes punctured easily and they were a nuisance. The racing sulky was about the only horse-drawn vehicle that used them.

The prime difficulty in the whole tire trade was fastening the tires to the rims. The clincher principle was popular for a time. In this the rubber was held in a steel channel by converging flanges, but it was not entirely satisfactory. Following the clincher came the circumferential retaining wire idea for holding the tire to the rim. The idea had several variations; the scheme was to imbed wires in the rubber near the base of the tire and clamp to these wires, but the plan was practical only for small sizes, and there was a great deal of trouble with the wires cutting through the rubber and permitting the body of the tire to loosen and come off the rim. Each company had its own particular style of fastening, but none was entirely satisfactory.

49

James A. Sweinhart of Akron had invented a tire which he claimed overcame most of the difficulties of fastening the tire to the rim. His idea was not new to me; I had heard of it in Chicago—although I had never seen a set of his tires. He placed wires crosswise in the base of the tire with the ends projecting through on both sides between the flanges; then he sprung endless retaining wires over the edges of the flanges, catching and binding the ends of the cross wires. This held the tire securely in place. It was much the best device on the market, and it made possible the safe fastening of large tires, whereas all the other devices failed completely in the larger sizes. Sweinhart had several men interested with him. Among them were Dr. L. E. Sisler, the county auditor; M. D. Buckman, one of his deputies; and James Christy, Jr., who was a builder. None of these men knew anything about practical tire making, and they were in no position financially or otherwise to go into the tire business. Sweinhart himself had been a schoolteacher but was then a carpenter building and selling houses on speculation. His real estate transactions brought him in contact with Doctor Sisler, whom he finally persuaded to become interested in organizing a company.

Sweinhart had already been around to most of the rubber people and had been turned down. He was told that his device was not practical—that the jolting would loosen the cross wires and the turning out of the street-car tracks would pull off the tires. Doctor Sisler tried the objections out before he agreed to go in with Sweinhart. He had a tired wheel put under a trip hammer and pounded for an hour or two; then he bought an old phaeton, had Sweinhart equip it with tires, and had a man driving it around town for a week with explicit directions to turn suddenly out of the streetcar tracks whenever he had the chance. The tires stood the tests.

Doctor Sisler did not know me, but he knew a pair of sorrels that I drove and he knew that I was a newcomer in town and interested in tire making. A man used to be judged by the horses he drove, and Doctor Sisler thought mine were a bit better than his—which qualified me as the man to push the patent. He called me on the telephone, introduced himself, and asked me if I should be interested in Sweinhart's tire. I told him I should be interested. "If that's so, I think we had better get together," he went on.

"All right, make it this evening," I answered.

That evening—it was the twenty-sixth of July, 1900—I met with Doctor Sisler, Christy, Buckman, and Sweinhart at Christy's house. Sweinhart's patent was about a year old, and its validity had already been tested in a suit by the India Rubber Company for infringement. We had no trouble at all in coming to terms, and signed an agreement that day.

By this agreement we were to organize a company with a capital of $50,000. I put in $10,000 in cash and my option on the tire business of the company for which I received an additional

$15,000 worth of stock. The other group put in $10,000 in cash and the Sweinhart patent, and received an additional $15,000 in stock, which gave us a working capital of $20,000. I was to be manager of the company at a salary of $3,000 a year with a bonus of $600 if the company earned 20 percent or more on its issued capital stock during the first year. Our hopes were larger than our experience; I never got my bonus. On the third of August, 1900, a charter was issued to us in West Virginia, creating the Firestone Tire & Rubber Company, and we organized according to the terms of the agreement, with James Christy, Jr., as president; J. A. Sweinhart as vice-president; L. E. Sisler, secretary; and H. S. Firestone, treasurer and general manager. The directors were Firestone, Christy, Sweinhart, Miller (my lawyer), and A. P. Cleveland, our first salesman. I did not want to be president, and in fact did not become president until three years later. I have never cared much about titles—it did not bother me who had the title so long as I ran the company.

I cannot say that the new tire company was particularly welcome in Akron. The big rubber companies thought that there were already enough people making tires, but, at the same time, we were so small that they did not bother their heads much about us—and we did not manufacture. For two years we practically did a jobbing business, having our tires made in Akron, and for a new company we were very successful. In the first year we sold $110,000 worth of tires and in the second year we sold $150,000 worth. This was too much business for a company with only $20,000 in cash, and we were soon ahead of our capital, and to my duties as general manager, general salesman, and general everything I had to add that of stock salesman. We increased our capitalization first to $150,000 and later to $200,000 because it became evident that before long we should either have to do our own manufacturing or go out of business.

It was at this time that S. G. Carkhuff, our present secretary, came with us as a bookkeeper. I hired him myself, persuading him to take a lower wage than he had been receiving from the Washburn-Crosby Company. But as yet we scarcely had an organization. We did not need any. Our only essential equipment was a simple machine for springing the wire bands over the projecting lugs of the tires. We could not afford to carry stocks of any size. We sold to carriage makers and carriage dealers. They sent us their wheels, we fitted them with steel channels to hold the tires, had the tires made, sprung the retaining wires into place, and returned the wheels. There was nothing at all complicated about the business or its finance, excepting that we did not have money enough to swing our volume of operations—and not having enough money is always complicated!

Our margin of profit was very narrow at the best, and at the worst we lost money. For three years we lost money on operations as a whole, but this did not bother me as to the eventual success of the enterprise, because I knew how and why we lost our money. Losing money is not pleasant, but every business must at times lose money. Losing money is really serious if you do not know why you are losing, or if you do know why and cannot help yourself. It was very plain to me why we were losing money. Only a miracle could have taken us out of red.

We had the best tire-fastening device on the market; our tires stayed on better than any of the others. But the very tire manufacturers who were our competitors in the open market were also the manufacturers of our tires. They made ample profits in selling to us, but we in turn could not ask much of a profit from our customers else we should have had our prices far too high. We could not offer a better tire than any one else—that would have been absurd on the face of things, for we were not making our tires—we were buying them from companies which also sold tires. Therefore our price was regulated by the merit of our patent—and while it had merit in plenty, it could not command a luxury price. We wanted to sell tires, not jewels.

That is why it became imperative for us to do our own manufacturing. Against the setting up of a plant stood the financial difficulty. I sold the 6 percent mortgage of $20,000 which I had designed as a $1,200 annuity for life. My whole $45,000 was soon in the stock in the company, and I was on the hunt day and night for men to buy our stock. It was no easy matter to sell stock in a company that had no assets excepting a patent on which it was losing money. For years I never saw a man with money without turning over in my mind how I could transfer some of his money into our stock. I did some bank borrowing in Akron, Massillon, and some of the smaller towns such as Canal Dover, where either Doctor Sisler or I was acquainted, but it was not bank credit but stock subscriptions that we then needed—money that did not have to be paid back. It would have been sheer suicide to go into a capital extension like a new factory on short-time bank credit.

And I did sell stock! The one man in particular to whom I wanted to sell I could not reach, and that was Will Christy. He was the biggest man in Akron and probably the most influential man in Ohio. He was then president of the Central Savings & Trust Company of Akron, and had become very wealthy in the construction of electric street railways. He was among the builders of the first electric railway, and he built the first interurban road in the country—that between Akron and Cleveland. He was just the man to give us financial tone and respectability, and following my old sales policy of going out after the big fellows, I laid my plans to sell Will Christy.

The trouble was I could not get to him. He had a big office and secretaries and all the usual safeguards of a busy man, and I could not get past those guards. The fact that he was a brother of James Christy, who was already in the company, did not help at all. Of course, I might have tried him at his house in the evening, but that would have been poor policy. A man of affairs does not want to be bothered in the evening. A great many salesmen make the mistake of thinking that pestering a man is the same as selling him, and they get their prospects into such a state of exasperation that they would not buy a gold dollar from them at 50 percent off. Just getting to a man is not enough—it is when and how you get to him. There are more wrong times to sell to a man that there are right times, and if I ever should write a book on salesmanship I should give about one third of the book to the topic "Common Sense." I have been buttonholed thousands of times by salesmen who, if they had just exercised a grain of common sense, would have known that, while the moment might be a very good one in which to make my acquaintance, it was no time at all to persuade me buy anything.

A good salesman will never intrude. In the first place, he will know that intruders do not make sales, and in the second place he will have to have brains enough to arrange for the right kind of meeting with his prospect—no man likes to be panhandled, and some selling comes to close to panhandling.

I kept tab on Will Christy's plans, and I learned that he was going to California with his wife for a vacation of several months. I found that he was going to stop over at the Auditorium Hotel in Chicago on his way out, and I took a train ahead of his to Chicago, registered at the hotel, made certain that Mr. and Mrs. Christy had registered later in the evening, and made equally certain that they did not see me that evening, for I already knew Mr. Christy slightly. The next morning I was up very early and kept out of sight until I saw Mr. and Mrs. Christy going in for breakfast. Quite by accident, of course, I met them at the door of the dining room.

We had breakfast together. He inquired about our business. One thing led naturally to another, and before breakfast was over he had bought $10,000 worth of stock. Later, Mr. Christy bought around $50,000 worth of our stock, became our president, and was of immense help to us at a time when we needed all the help we could get.

And he sold himself! All I did was to fall in with him at the right time.

56 "A soundly financed business ought to have enough free money of its own to be out of the banks during the dull period of the year and reserve its bank borrowing for the busy seasons."

Chapter V
The First Profits

We had to have a new factory, and we had precious little money to spend. We got the factory, and we spent precious little money. It came about this way.

I noticed an abandoned foundry building at Sweitzer and Miller avenues in South Akron—which was then out in the country. It was a single-story tile building about one hundred by seventy-five feet, and nearby was a little wooden shack which would do very well for an office. Most of the windows had been broken, weeds were growing luxuriously all about—a dismal monument to a dream that did not come true. However, at the moment, I was not thinking of writing an elegy—I was looking for a cheap factory site. And surely this one ought to be cheap enough. And it was.

The defunct foundry had been liquidated by the Second National Bank, which was, so we discovered, extremely anxious to get rid of the property. Doctor Sisler and I saw Fred Smith, the president of the bank. He said the bank ought to have $4,500 for the place—which was a fair enough price.

"When do you want your money?" I asked.

"Whenever you can pay," he answered.

He took our personal notes in part for the purchase price and never pressed us for payment of the notes. The next step was to make the building habitable, and after that to turn it into a tire factory, and this we managed to get through on very little money. My uncle Mahlin Erwin was foreman for the Buckeye Engine Company in Salem, Ohio, and he picked up for us, second-hand, a 125-horsepower Buckeye engine for $2,200 and then erected it for us for nothing. I bought a couple of 125-horse-power boilers in excellent condition for $1,800, got

a washer for $850, two mills for $2,500, and also I found a vulcanizer at a bargain. This was the minimum equipment for washing and mixing preparatory to vulcanizing the finished tire. We already had moulds, and while we should have had a calender (which is the name of the machine that coats the fabric with rubber), since the only fabric then used in a solid tire was a strip fastened at the base, we managed to get along for a year buying our fabric already calendered. Then I bought a second-hand calender for $2,000—it would have cost more than twice that amount new.

We did not have a single new piece of machinery in that factory except a mill and washer and two boilers. Nevertheless, we had a well-equipped plant for its size, for the machinery was just as good as new. My son Harvey, then five years old, turned on the steam and we were off for better or for worse.

We had twelve men working only one day shift. I believe that a dozen better men have never been brought together. Among them were Alfred Wegmiller, who is still with us as the engineer of the clubhouse; and the McClisters, W. J. and Robert, both of whom have retired. A little later came Daniel Goodenberger and John Herget, both of whom are now in our solid-tire department. I was the superintendent of the factory, in addition to my other duties, and I was in the factory as much as I was in the office or on the road. I think it is absolutely necessary that a man should know how his goods are made, and although I have never set up as a rubber or tire expert, I do know how most operations ought to be carried through. This knowledge has stood me in good stead, for it very frequently happens that the best technical men have not in them the instinct of management, and if the man at the top is not a practical manager, then the benefits of technique will be lost. I have made it a point never to allow myself to be a curiosity in the shops. Nowadays, of course, I have nothing to do with the active shop management, but I get out through every department often enough to know pretty well what is going on, and what is more, I do not recall ever having made a trip through the shops without picking up something.

In the first little shop we had a foreman, but he was a working foreman, and it has been our practice since to have our foremen as far as possible on a working basis. I find that a working foreman usually has a better control over his men than a non-worker, because he has to be continually on his mettle to demonstrate that he is a better workman than any of them, and also he does not ask them to do the unreasonable things which some foremen will insist on. It was not the pay that attracted these men to us or made them work. They got only from ten to fifteen cents an hour, which was the prevailing rate. I have never found that pay alone would either bring together or hold good men. I think it was the game itself that drew these men; we were a little company fighting among big companies, and we were all together in the fight. I knew all the men well, not only in the factory but in their homes. Their affairs were our affairs, and our affairs were their affairs. Nobody thought much of hours or special duties or anything but the work. A man became a specialist in whatever his job at the moment happened to be. If we had a big order of tires to get out, it was no infrequent thing for a shift to keep right on until the work was done. None of us thought of overtime. We had no extra money to spend. Mr. Carkhuff, acting as bookkeeper, and I were in the office, and we had one stenographer, or, as we should now more grandly say, "secretary." Miss V. M. Greer was the second stenographer we hired and she also acted as assistant bookkeeper. She came to us fresh from a business college, and although I think her pay was to be only five dollars a week, we thought well and earnestly before we took on the new obligation. She has been with us ever since, and for many years now has been cashier. It was not that five dollars a week for Miss Greer would have broken us. We took on extra men in the factory without question whenever we needed them. But repair men and office employees are not strictly productive—that is, they produce indirectly, not directly. No employee who is really non-productive ought to be retained. It is much easier to check up on who is really needed in production than on who is really needed in the indirect labour, and hence, every addition to the indirect or overhead expense should be studied vigilantly. This is especially true in these days when luxuries so rapidly become necessities. An executive is the better off for having a comfortable desk and chair and a convenient place to work, and there is no reason why surroundings should not be good looking rather than ugly, but an office is essentially a place in which to work. It is not a club and it ought not to be fitted up as a club—else it may turn into a club. When a concern is earning large profits, an extra $10,000 spent in getting more elaborate office equipment seems a mere trifle, but no company always earns large profits, and there are times when $10,000 looks big to almost any company. And there is more satisfaction in having the ten in bank than in having it in a row of ornate chairs!

Our volume of orders developed satisfactorily. In 1903, we did a total business of $230,000 as against somewhat over $100,000 two years before. Our payroll was not large, but in those days we used wild rubber from Brazil, and while its quality was uneven (which frequently involved us in manufacturing difficulties), the price was more uneven than the quality. The fluctuating prices of rubber in recent years have frequently put the whole tire-making industry in a precarious condition, but in those days rubber regularly fluctuated between a dollar and three dollars a pound, because the whole quantity of rubber arriving was so small as compared with present-day consumption that it did not take much money to manipulate the market. In general, it does not pay for anyone to buy raw materials in advance of legitimate manufacturing requirements, but in a manipulated market, a man with money can beat the game by buying when the price is low. That we did not have the money to do; we had our hands full buying rubber to fill our orders; we bought in carload lots, paying one third cash, one third in sixty, and one third in ninety days, and it was no easy matter to meet these payments.

Will Christy became president to help our credit, and he endorsed notes up to a limit of, I think, $15,000, which was a great help at the time, because his standing was unquestioned, but afterward, when we needed much larger sums, the endorsement was a positive detriment, for, naturally, all the banks wanted the paper that he endorsed, and there was not enough of it to go around. I also endorsed and kept on endorsing for years, until the company got on its feet, and while at the beginning my endorsement was really little more than sentimental, because everything I had was in company and if it fell I should fall, too, yet it was a guarantee of good faith to the banks. In later years, when we began to borrow large sums, my endorsement was of no particular value to the banks, because the amount of paper outstanding was commonly far beyond my personal fortune. But even at that, I had a great deal of trouble in getting off the paper.

It was during this period that I made the acquaintance of Edward S. Lacey, who had been in the Treasury Department and was then president of the Metropolitan National Bank of Chicago. I just dropped in on him one day while in Chicago to see if I could open a line of credit. I had no introduction or references, and he had never heard of me, but he very quickly became interested in my story of the business and what I thought it was going to do. He liked our policy of not declaring dividends. In the year 1903, we had earned a profit for the first time—we earned $8,503. Some of the stockholders thought we at once ought to declare a dividend in order to make the sale of stock easier, but that policy I steadily opposed, as also I opposed the sale of any stock below par. I bought my own stock at par, and I bought every share I could. For ten years I lived in a rented house at $40 a month, in order to put my money back into stock. Mr. Lacey liked these ideas; he was an extremely conservative man, but at that first meeting, which must have lasted several hours, he gave us a $15,000 line of credit, and thereafter, every year for many years, I spent at least half a day with him, going over the affairs of the company in detail preparatory to renewing our line of credit. He was always afraid we would go too fast, but he believed in us, and I prize a letter from him, written by hand in 1914, when he was a very old man, asking me if I knew where he could buy some of our preferred stock. At that time he was chairman of the advisory committee of the Continental & Commercial Bank of Chicago, which had taken over his bank. I took no important step of any kind during these early years without first consulting with Mr. Lacey, and, although I did not always follow his advice, because he was inclined to be too conservative, yet I never failed to get a great deal from him and avoided many pitfalls. We never, during this period, although we needed money desperately for additional equipment, borrowed for fixed capital. We owed for our factory, it is true, in the form of ninety-day notes, but these notes were not really due in ninety days—they were to be paid off only when we could afford it. A soundly financed business ought to have enough free money of its own to be out of the banks during the dull period of the year and reserve its bank borrowing for the busy seasons. I cannot too greatly emphasize or repeat too many times that bank borrowing for any capital purpose is asking for more luck than falls to the ordinary enterprise. Buildings and tools and machinery cannot be expected to pay for themselves in three months, or six months, or a year. Short-term, capital borrowing has to be repaid either out of profits or out of the sale of capital assets—which means liquidation. This is not taking depreciation into account at all, and also it takes no account of the narrow second-hand market for special machinery. Even if I buy a standard machine, it is a second-hand machine the moment after I buy it, and at least the seller's profit has to be deducted. It took us some years to get on a really sound financial basis. We always got out of each bank once a year, but it was a long time before we could get out of all of our banks at the same time. We had to shift our loans to make our clean-ups, and although this was perfectly satisfactory to the banks, it was not satisfactory to me. I have always liked to have the work in hand fully to liquidate the bank credit.

The big rubber companies, as I have said, did not particularly welcome a new rubber company in Akron. We were more or less tolerated before we had our factory, because then we had to buy from the other companies, but once we began to manufacture, the attitude toward us distinctly changed. The big companies could make lower prices on tires on account of the volume of business they did in all kinds of rubber goods, while we made only tires. I was immediately faced with this question:

"Will you cut your quality, reduce prices, and meet competition, or will you try to sell at your present price?"

That question was not a poser. It answered itself. We could not, with our facilities, lower our prices and still earn a profit. If our tires were better than any others manufactured, and I believed they were, then we could sell them at a price higher than our competitors charged. The public is always willing to pay for quality. If we were just fooling ourselves about the quality being better, then the public would not pay us an extra price and we should fail. The real test was of product. Cutting the quality was urged on me, but it did not impress me as being an alternative. If we lowered our quality and frankly turned out poor tires, then we should eventually have to fail, because no one making and selling what he knows to be a poor thing can hope to continue to succeed. It all gets around to the service you are trying to render. I believe in keeping prices low, for, regardless of service, there is no real profit in high prices, because high prices automatically cut down volume. But the only possible way to lower prices and still keep business is to save in the cost of manufacturing by improved processes. Quality must go up, not down, and if a competitor lowers his quality, that is exactly the time for you to raise yours. Our competitors did not lower their qualities—they did not have to do that in order to get under our prices, for their manufacturing facilities were better and their volume so much larger than ours. We met the test; we were selling the highest-priced tire on the market, but our sales kept up steadily. We were not put out of business. Competition rarely puts anyone out of business—a man usually puts himself out of business either by not making a good article or by wrong methods in sales or finance.

However, we did not long have to bother about prices, for we quickly developed a tire that put us out of competition. All the carriage-tire manufacturers made them exactly one way—that is, by what was known as the "single cure" process. Each length of tire was moulded for the wheel it was designed to fit, and then cured separately. The carriage wheels of the day had at least ten different diameters, and hence, any dealer who held himself out as prepared to do business had to carry a minimum of four hundred tires. Nothing was standardized; a wheel of a given diameter might have any one of ten cross sections, according to the whim of the maker. It had often been suggested that if only tires could be made in continuous lengths, then the dealers would have to stock only the various cross sections, and simply by cutting off a sufficient length of the right cross section, could fit any diameter of wheel. The idea was simple enough, but so many practical difficulties about curing came up that tire manufacturers generally had agreed that the plan was not practicable and had given up the attempt to do the obvious.

We had an employee by the name of George Ludington, who felt that he could succeed where the others had failed. I went to work with him, and we developed an absolutely practical tire which we sold in rolls to be cut off and made into tires by the dealer. The technical details of just how we did this are not interesting. From that time forward we sold tires in reels, just like hose. That invention took us completely out of competition; a dealer with a small stock of our roll tires was better equipped to serve his customers than if he had a big stock of our competitors' completed tires. We developed a good many other specialties. We had special steel channels rolled that gave better service than the ordinary trade channels. The "side-wire" device permitted us to go into the automobile and truck field, because it was the only device which would hold a heavy tire firmly in place. We equipped practically the whole fleet of the Parmalee Company of Chicago with the heavy tires, and we also essayed into even larger tires. We made one eight inches wide, which, in addition to the side wires, had a wire through the centre. The most noteworthy fact about this tire is that it took our entire factory force to put it on a wheel!

We developed something of an export trade, but our first venture nearly ended in disaster. José Alvarez y Cía, of Havana, Cuba, had heard of our side-wire tire and placed an order with us through New York. Just about the time we were looking anxiously for a draft, we got a letter from the company denouncing our tires, refusing to pay for them, and asking what we were going to do about it. We desperately needed the money, but more than that, we needed the goodwill. I guessed that the Cubans had somehow gone wrong in attaching the tires. It was not a case for writing letters—and anyway, I think the best way to settle trouble is face to face. I could not go to Cuba, so I asked Mr. Carkhuff to go down. I suspected that the Cubans had broken the machines for attaching the rims and tires, and although Mr. Carkhuff was not a factory man and probably had never attached a tire in his life, we furnished him with a set of machines and started him off. To meet this emergency, it was necessary for him to get into the factory immediately, don a pair of overalls, and apply himself to the job at hand.

When Mr. Carkhuff arrived in Havana, he found the Custom House closed for two weeks for the inauguration of the first president of Cuba—and all his attaching machinery, as well as a supply of tires, was in the Custom House. Somehow, he got them through and then went to meet Señor Alvarez. The Señor thought that he had been made a fool of. Mr. Carkhuff, talking through an interpreter, managed to get his consent to look at the tires that had given all the trouble. Just as we thought, the Cuban workmen had misread the instructions, broken the attaching machine, and, of course, put the tires on all wrong. Mr. Carkhuff set up his machine, put on the tires properly, and invited Senor Alvarez to give them a trial—and a trial he did give them. The Señor brought out a pair of his best horses, and with Carkhuff trembling beside him, drove wildly all over the town, turning out of car tracks at full speed and dashing around corners on two wheels, like a madman. The tires held, Carkhuff held, and when it was all over the Señor asked for an exclusive contract for our tires in Cuba, at the same time guaranteeing a minimum sale. This company has represented us in Cuba ever since, and for a time was our largest single customer. This loyalty has resulted in our mutual prosperity. I understand that once, when a competitor attempted, without a license, to sell a tire much like ours, the Señor, instead of enduring the tedium of an infringement suit, had the competitor thrown into jail and kept there until he promised to be good.

A big change was coming over the tire industry. It was one that I had to be in on, and yet, for the moment, I saw no way of getting in. We had built up our business in solid tires principally for carriages and electric automobiles. But now the gasoline automobile was coming forward rapidly, and for these the pneumatic tire was unquestionably the best. We made cushion tires, but they were practically solid tires. If I read the signs correctly, solid tires would soon be a minor product. We did not know how to make pneumatic tires, but we could learn. This was more serious; the pneumatic-tire industry was already sewn up tight in a patent association which was not granting any more business to manufacturers. That is what we were up against.

68   " There is always a better way of doing everything than the way which is standard at the moment. "

Chapter VI
Starting in the Pneumatic Tire Business

The shift in the tire industry from solids to pneumatics began just as we were counting ourselves successful. Our sales
for 1904 were $460,000, precisely double those of the previous
year, while our profits were $71,043, which is a pretty respecta-
ble earning on a capital of $200,000, and nearly nine times the
profit of the previous year. Nevertheless, I was determined to
take on the manufacture of pneumatic tires, which we knew
nothing about and where a hard fight awaited us.

The easy course was to take for granted that, having established
a fair solid-tire business, that business would expand and continue, and there would be no need to go into new fields. But
the gasoline car was developing rapidly—although only Mr.
Ford at that time had any notion that the automobile would
be what it is today. It seemed to me inevitable that the automobile would come into wide use. That would mean an enormous tire requirement, and these tires would be pneumatics.
By no means all our stockholders agreed with me, and one man
holding a large block of stock disagreed in so personal a way
that I had to arrange to buy out his stock. I saw clearly that, if
we limited ourselves to solid tires, our business would slowly
die. No business can succeed unless it is constantly revising its
product, not only to meet the actual demands of today but also
the potential demands of tomorrow.

A product can never really be standardized—that is not in
the nature of things. The real point is that changes should not
be made lightly or for catch-penny purposes. They should be
made only to improve convenience or durability or appear-
ance. Some changes may be made in the interests of more
economical manufacturing, but this is dangerous ground, for
it may lead one into thinking more of the factory than of the
public. I had not in mind making any sudden shift to pneumatic-tire production, because we had plenty of solid-tire business.

It was the future I had to provide for. The outstanding difficulty with the pneumatic tire was in holding it on the rim—just as it had been the outstanding difficulty with the solid tire. That a tire might be made hollow and filled with compressed air had been known for a long time. The first patent for a pneumatic tire was issued as early as 1845, but it was not until 1888 that John B. Dunlop of Belfast, Ireland, took out a patent for a double-tube tire. He wanted to help his boy win a tricycle race. He inflated a rubber tube and put over it a jacket or casing of Irish linen. After the inner tube was placed in position and inflated, it was held in by lacing the jacket, and the tire was held to a flat wooden rim by flaps coated with rubber cement. Then Jeffery brought out a pneumatic tire secured to an especially constructed rim by metal hooks, while, a year or two later, P. W. Tillinghast brought out the single-tube bicycle tire which was the tire most generally used on bicycles. Some time later, an important patent was issued for a thicker and tougher tread; up until then, tires did not have treads as we now know them. The tire was simply a round piece of rubber tubing of as nearly even strength and thickness as the skill of the makers would permit.

When the automobile began to come in, the manufacturers used modifications of the bicycle tire to which they had been most accustomed. In America, we had the single tube, in England, the wired-on double tube, and in France, the clincher double-tube type. Gradually, all came around to the clincher, soft-bead, doubletube tire, and between 1900 and 1905 the clincher tire was perfected in America. In the early years, however, each maker had his own design of clincher tires and rims, and it was not until 1903 that the manufacturers agreed to standardize on the contours of tires and rims so that they would be interchangeable.

The clincher method of fastening had become standard. And what was supposed to be the basic patent covering every form of clincher construction was held by the "G. & J. Clincher Tire Association." The scheme was in analogy to the Selden patent organization, under which all the domestic automobile manufacturers, with the exception of Mr. Ford, were working. The delusion that monopoly is profitable had not then died out.

Under the Selden patent, the manufacture of automobiles was a tight monopoly. The Clincher Tire Association not only monopolized the making of clincher tires, but allotted the production. It issued licenses to manufacturers with a stipulation covering the percentage each might make during a year. The prices of all tires were rigidly fixed, and the profits of any production beyond the allotted percentage had to be turned back into the pool. This pooling and price regulating notion is a curious one. Every one of the tire makers was financially strong and completely able to take care of himself. The pneumatic tire demand was not large, for the general public had not yet started buying motor cars—they had not reached the farm. But if the Association had fully succeeded in its aims and had continued to monopolize pneumatic tire making, it would greatly have retarded the industry. If both the clincher-tire patent and the Selden patent had held, we could not have had the automobile industry of today. It would have kept the motor industry in the pleasure and sporting class until the monopoly had run its course. The new age of transport would have been delayed. And, of course, the tire industry would have had to jog along behind. It could not make more sets of tires than there were cars to put them on.

I asked the Association for a license and was refused. But since I had determined to go into the making of pneumatic tires, I looked around for some method of fastening them to the rims which would not involve me in litigation with the powerful Association. I had no money to spend on lawsuits, while the Association had a big legal battery ready to open fire at the mere suggestion of infringement. I found a man with a device which seemed to me to be practical, although its construction was very crude. It was essentially the same as the straight-side tire of today: the rim had the side rings or flanges bolted together. The principle was far better than that of the clincher tire, and it has developed into the straight-side tire of today. But I took it up, not because I thought it was better than the clincher, but because I could not get permission to build the clincher. It is a curious coincidence that both the side-wire solid tire and the straight-side pneumatic tire proved to be the only methods for fastening on the heavy tires that were to come. But I was forced, as an outsider, into both of them! There is always a better way

71

of doing everything than the way which is standard at the moment. It is a good thing for a man to be pushed into finding that better way.

The making of pneumatic tires is entirely different from the making of solid tires; the solid tire is moulded and the pneumatic tire is built up on a core. I hired a tire maker, put him in a corner of the shop, and started him making pneumatic tires by hand. We had no automobile on which to try them out, so I went to New York, bought a Maxwell at Tarrytown, and shipped it out by express. Its wheels were arranged for the standard clincher tires, and we had to fit on new rims and flanges, turned out in a local machine shop. These flanges gave us no end of trouble, and we were several months getting a set of tires and flanges that would stay put. Then I set out to drive to the old home at Columbiana, or rather started out with a mechanic driving, because I did not then know how to manage an automobile. We left early in the morning, and it was half-past three in the afternoon before we reached Columbiana—a distance of sixty miles. Most of that time we spent monkeying with the tires. Every few feet—at least, that is how it now seems—we had a blowout. The tires stayed on well enough; the trouble was with the shape of the rim. The side flange did not fit close enough to keep the inner tube from being pinched and punctured.

Eventually, I reached the old farm, went over to the picnic grounds, and held a kind of reception. It was the first automobile that most of the people had seen, and I had a lot of fun giving them rides.

That initial demonstration of what we could do with pneumatic tires might have been taken as conclusive proof that we did not know anything about them. We did not need any proof of that fact. I did not pretend to know anything about pneumatics—I was trying to learn. We kept busy for a year learning how better to make the rims and the tires, until at last we had a fairly satisfactory product. Then we were ready to go on the market. But there was no market to go on.

Every automobile in the country was fitted to take clincher tires, and in order to sell a set of our tires, we had to convince an owner that ours were so much better than any of the others that he would be warranted in changing his rims and for ever tying himself to us, for our straight-side tires could not be used on the clincher rim, and the clincher tires could not be used on our rim. Our tires were better than the other tires.

The clincher-tire people knew the arguments against our tire even better than we did. We could sell only an occasional set of tires, and yet we had to get into the pneumatic-tire business.

In 1905, I learned that Henry Ford intended to build two thousand cars to sell at $500 and therefore would need two thousand sets of tires. There was an opening for our tires, for if I could induce him to put out these cars with our rims, then we should have two thousand customers who would have to use our tires to the exclusion of all others. I packed off at once to Detroit and put my proposal before Mr. Ford. I outlined the principle of my tire and its mechanical advantages. The tire combination thought all the business must come to them, anyway. There was no competition at all between members. They had made Mr. Ford a price of $70 a set. I made a price of $55, which was enough to give me an adequate profit.

This was my first business meeting with Mr. Ford. The Ford Motor Company was manufacturing several styles of cars, and although the cars were being built according to Mr. Ford's designs, practically all the parts were made outside. He told me that they would soon go into manufacturing on a large scale. None of us knew very much about pneumatic tires, and Mr. Ford, after an initial examination of my tire, seemed willing to leave the tire question to me. He was wholly interested in getting out a car that he could sell at a low price. He spoke a little of his complete conviction that the automobile was not a mere pleasure conveyance but a new form of transportation, and that the price had to be brought down to a point where any one could afford to buy. It was the engine—the heart of the automobile—that held his attention. Tires were just incidental.

We had a common bond. The Ford Company was being prosecuted vigorously under the Selden patent, and Mr. Ford mentioned how foolish it was for any group of manufacturers to imagine they could monopolize an immense transportation industry. I also was outside the favoured ring, for I was not permitted to make clincher tires. Perhaps being in the same boat had some weight, for Mr. Ford was anxious to break away from the tire monopoly.

"If your tire proves to be what you think it is, then we'll use it," said Mr. Ford finally.

It is a characteristic of Mr. Ford's that, no matter how perfect any mechanical device may seem on paper, he will accept it only after the most rigid tests. I had a couple of Ford cars fitted with our tires, and for sixty days these cars were driven through the roads and streets. The tires stood every test.

I left Detroit with an order for 2,000 sets of tires in my pocket. Fortunately, they were not to be delivered all at once, but even at that, the order was a sizable one for a little concern like ours that had never sold many pneumatic tires. It seems to me highly probable that if we had really known anything about pneumatic tires, the order would have been neither given nor taken. That order was the biggest job I had yet undertaken, for our pneumatic-tire department consisted of one man. We had to organize a department, we had to get the rims made, and, above all, we had to finance the order.

As a starter, I borrowed $5,000, but right away I struck a snag in the side flanges to hold on the tires. Those which we had used in our experiments had been made by hand, and they were expensive, clumsy, and not very strong. We knew almost nothing of special steels, and, of course, we had no facilities for experimenting. The best arrangement I could make with the local company was at $20 a set, and hardly had they started in to build before I found that they did not know what they were doing, and if we depended on them for our rims, we should surely fall down on our contract. I found another company which could make first-class rims in an electric welding process for $15 a set, which meant the difference between a profit and a loss to us on the whole Ford contract. The first company, in spite of the fact that it could not make satisfactory flanges, wanted to keep on, and I nearly had a lawsuit on my hands.

Settling disputes through the law has never appealed to me as a pastime. Lawsuits are not only extremely expensive, but they do not and cannot settle anything which could not be better and more quickly settled through putting all the cards on the table and having a frank talk. A man who wants justice does not often have to go to the courts to get it. In fact, he will compromise with something less than justice to keep out of court. A fair man is drawn into court only when the other side refuses to face the facts. I avoided a lawsuit with this first flange-making company by going to the president and saying:

"You and I know all the facts, and we ought to be able to make a better settlement than any judge and jury, because they will only know such facts as we tell them. And in addition to that, we shall have our lawyers to pay. If we go to law, we shall drag along for several years, and in the end, no matter which one of us gets the verdict, both of us will lose. Why not put everything right down on paper now and strike a balance?"

In that way, we settled our differences. In the meantime, we had been gathering tire makers, buying fabric and rubber, and going ahead with the order. When we had built three hundred of the tires, the Ford Company told me that the new model would not be out for some months. The blow nearly knocked us flat. The three hundred tires alone represented a cash outlay of more than $10,000—most of which was borrowed money— while we had to keep on receiving the balance of the order for flanges, which meant a further outlay of around $25,000. The additional rubber ordered could be used in our solid-tire making, so that did not greatly bother us, while the fabric we had contracted for was not a serious item. But tying up $10,000 with the prospect of eventually having $35,000 tied up was staggering. It meant the wiping out of most of the money we expected to do business on.

We did not have enough bank credit to cover this contract and also continue our other operations. I had planned that around $15,000 in borrowed money would see us through, for the tires were to be paid for as delivered. It was close going. I renewed some of our notes as they came due. We put back our profits—which for 1905 amounted to $122,000—and I sold more stock. It would seem that with profits of this size the Ford order should not have embarrassed us, but our sales for that year were $770,000—almost double those of the year before. Our 12 men had grown to 130.

Our turnover was not very rapid, and hence this volume of business required a lot of ready money. Our profits were book profits, not cash profits. They were all ploughed right back into the business. Our capital remained at $200,000, but in five years of operation (for we scarcely got under way in 1900) we had not only paid off the heavy losses of two years, but had accumulated a surplus of more than $100,000. Anyone who has been connected with a fast-growing business knows what a pull it is to provide the money. We kept every free dollar moving as fast as we could. Had I known in advance that our big order was going to be held up, I should have managed my finances differently, but I had learned from my experience with banks carefully to forecast all financial requirements so that no promises would be made which could not be kept, and no emergency financing at high rates would have to be pushed through.

Although I have often needed money, I have never, not even during the financial crisis of 1920–21, been forced into paying exorbitant rates of interest. My bother with money has rarely been for the needs of today—it has been usually for a period two or three months away. The Ford contract and the unexpected increase in the solid-tire business upset the schedule that I had so carefully worked out. I began reaching out for more credit and opened additional bank accounts.

There was a considerable reluctance at that time among bankers to finance anybody or anything connected with the automobile industry. The bankers were almost unanimous in believing that the automobile was a passing fancy and would come and go just the way the bicycle had. The industry was not in a very good condition. Most of the concerns turning out automobiles only assembled parts that they bought, and a good many of them were not only working on small capital but really knew little about assembling, so that the machines gave a great deal of trouble.

The science of automobile engineering was only developing, and little was done on a really scientific basis. It is a fortunate thing for the industry that it was not favoured by the bankers, else it would have been financed by bond issues, and there have been several periods when these bond issues might have been foreclosed—which would have set back the industry for a number of years. The strength of the industry is that it has mostly been built out of money subscribed for stock or from profits reinvested in the business. I doubt if, at that time, I could have opened my line of banking credit had it not been that, with the exception of the Ford contract, all of my business was in solid tires for carriages. The banking opinion was that the horse would never be displaced.

In 1906 the Ford Motor Company began to take delivery. The tires we made under that contract were good tires. They were large and tough and gave fine service. Mr. Ford was immensely pleased with them, and we founded a connection which has never been broken and which has been of immeasurable help to us in many ways, but most particularly in the steady pressure for higher service and lower prices that keeping the contract has involved.

I scarcely believe that our company could ever have drifted into a condition of complete, non-thinking self-satisfaction. It is not in my disposition to stop and pin medals on myself. But any one who does business with Mr. Ford never gets a chance to rest and enjoy honours. The pressure for better methods is continuous. Of this more later.

The tires delivered to the Ford Company were, as I said, entirely satisfactory; but when the cars got out in use, we ran up against a trouble that none of us had really considered. Those cars could use only my tires, and I was not big enough to have branches and stations all over the country. I could not supply the users, and people did not want to buy cars for which they could not get new tires. The Ford Company said that I would have to make clincher tires. They wanted to do business with me. I either had to make clincher tires or quit the pneumatic-tire business. I went again to the head of the tire monopoly and renewed my application for a license. The president explained how much he would like to give me a license and how sorry he was that he could not, and so on.

"If you will not give me a license," I said, "then I will go right ahead and make clincher tires without a license."

And I did.

80 " If a man comes to you for the single reason that you offer him more money than he has been getting, he is not worth having, for then he is thinking too much of the money and too little of the job."

Chapter VII
The Development of the Industry

I looked for a lawsuit and a deal of trouble of various sorts from this going into the making of clincher tires without a license. I was mentally, if not financially, prepared for a long fight. The Selden suit against the Ford Motor Company had helped to sell the Ford car; when the Selden association were advertising that they intended to prosecute every owner of a Ford car, the company went to some expense to provide an indemnity bond which any purchaser might have for the asking—and so few purchasers asked for the bonds that it was not worthwhile keeping up the arrangement! The public always roots for the underdog.

I went on with my manufacturing, expecting every day to receive notice to quit, which would mean that the fight was on. I never got the notice. Not a soul bothered me. The tire association was concentrating on another infringement suit, and before the year was out, they lost that suit. The clincher tire patent was declared invalid, and any one who liked might make clincher tires. It was a great thing for the industry to be freed from this monopoly, but another monopoly was shortly to take its place.

The year 1906 was our big year. We reached the million mark in sales; Ford was already making more motor cars than any other manufacturer, and we had the larger part of their business. Our profits were $10,000 less than the year before, but they were large enough to increase the demand for a dividend to such a point that it could no longer be refused. I could not avoid paying dividends without a serious breach with some of my stockholders. But I did not want to weaken our cash position—we had too much business ahead and too many demands for money. So I compromised. We issued $100,000 additional stock, bringing our total capital up to $300,000, and allotted the new stock on the basis of one share for each two already held and to be paid for in instalments. Then we declared a 20 percent cash dividend to be applied to the stock purchase and a 2 percent cash dividend.

That was our first dividend. It helped to establish our stock, but that did not much interest me; I then and always have regarded the stock of our company as something to buy and hold and not something to speculate in. I have never bought a share on speculation—that is, with the intention of selling again. The moment that officers or directors of a company begin to speculate in its stock, the ruin of the company is not far away, for it is impossible to serve both the company and the stock market. Our stock had no market, and we made no effort to create one—the price of our stock did not concern us in the least. It was no easier to sell than ever it had been. For instance, we wanted to buy a small building adjoining our factory for an office. The price was around $5,000 and, not caring to let go any cash, I offered $1,000 cash and the balance in stock. The owner refused my offer; he wanted cash. If he had taken stock, he would be worth more than half a million today.

We made clincher tires for Ford, but also we made the straight-side tire. It soon became apparent that the straight-side method was the better for tires four inches and above, because a clincher tire of that size was hard to put on or take off, and with the frequent punctures of those days, taking off and putting on tires made up a fair part of the motorist's day. The need was then for a rim which, by reversing the flanges, would take either the clincher or the straight-side tire. We developed a detachable rim.

Each tire maker thought it necessary to have a rim of his own, but this brought on so much confusion that finally they pooled all their ideas and patents in a holding company, which was called the United Rim Company and which charged a royalty of two dollars a set. The manufacturers did not ask me to join the association—I was too small to bother with. But I should not have joined, for I had some rim ideas of my own, and anyway, I wanted to keep out of all price-fixing or royalty combinations. They did not impress me as being good business.

At a race meet, I noticed that the foreign cars had extra tires already mounted on rims for quick changing. That seemed an idea which need not be restricted to racing cars, and out of this grew our demountable rim. Things were stirring in the tire industry. It was really becoming an industry, because the making of automobiles was really becoming an industry. Fewer people were in the automobile "game" and more in the automobile "business." Tires were not as yet sold on a strictly business basis. No tire maker could guarantee his tires to go any certain mileage, because none of us knew how to manufacture tires to a uniform grade. There were several reasons for this. We did not know much about the properties of rubber, and every process in tire making was pretty much on the rule-of-thumb basis. We thought we knew a little about how a tire acted in service, but actually we knew nothing at all. It was a new science, and no one had developed a method for real investigation. We made our tires as we thought they ought to be made, but without any fund of exact knowledge to draw on. We had not yet investigated fabrics, and finally we used wild rubber from Brazil, and the quality of this varied widely. One lot of rubber would produce very good tires, while the next lot would produce very bad ones. The laboratory was not unknown to industry, but it was looked on as something of a luxury and not as the parent of profits. The large companies which manufactured a wide line of rubber products had laboratories, but I had not felt the need of one. I did not know how really important a laboratory was, and already having four or five places for every dollar that came in, I had no inclination to look for new ways of spending money. I did not know that the laboratory was at the very foundation of the tire industry.

83

Of course, the quality of solid tires had varied, but the strains on solid carriage tires were trifling as compared with those on pneumatic automobile tires, and a difference in rubber which, between two sets of carriage tires, would scarcely have mattered, made all the difference between a good automobile tire and a bad one. We had rough methods of testing our rubber, and they did well enough for the carriage tires, but automobile tires had to be exact. We could not have any guessing—we had to know. Only a chemist could know; therefore we had to have a chemist and a laboratory. I heard that a chemist by the name of John Thomas was well thought of. I asked him to visit me at my house some evening. He dropped in, and we had a talk. Before hiring a man, I like to talk to him in a general way—to talk a little about everything and nothing, and to find out what sort of a human being he is. For, first of all, an executive has to be human—a technical man who is only a technical man is valuable, but he cannot organize or head a department. I liked Thomas. I found that he was satisfied enough with his place, but that he was anxious to work into a position where he would have a greater opportunity to expand. He was just an employee in his department and had no opportunity to use executive or organizing ability. He was getting, so he told me, ninety dollars a month.

"Will you come with me and lay out a laboratory and take charge of it?" I asked. "And how much would you want?"

"I'd like to think it over," he answered. "But it seems to me I'd like to do it. However, I ought to have one hundred dollars a month."

"No," I answered, "we might as well decide it all right now, and I can't afford to pay you over ninety a month."

"If I have to decide, then I'll decide to come out, and I'll start at ninety dollars. I think there is a chance to do something."

"If that's the case," I continued, "then we'll make it one hundred dollars and call it a bargain!"

I will never bid a man away from a job. It is not fair to the man and it is not fair to his employer. If a man comes to you for the single reason that you offer him more money than he has been getting, he is not worth having, for then he is thinking too much of the money and too little of the job. Very often a man is underpaid in his job and perhaps treated unfairly in a number of ways. He may be in the kind of an organization in which there is no future; there may be a good many reasons why a man feels he ought to change his job. If such be the case, he ought to change his job, and he would be a fool if he made the change simply because the second job offered less money, but he would be almost as much of a fool if he changed simply because the second job offered more money. The money part cannot be put aside; everyone has to live, and there are unfortunately times when a man has to look solely to the pay, but from the employer's standpoint the really valuable man is the one who is willing to take the chance of eventually making himself worth a large salary.

Thomas organized a laboratory. It was not much of a laboratory—just a bit of the shop partitioned off. That laboratory opened my eyes to what science in manufacturing means. But that is a subject in itself. Thomas developed the department little by little, spending only small sums of money, until it became the powerful experiment and technical control station of today. I would almost as soon try to make tires without rubber as to try to make them without a chemist.

Now Thomas is the vice-president of the company: he added executive ability to technical ability.

Not long after Thomas came with us, he and I made a most extraordinary trip together. A man in a small town in Ohio claimed to have discovered a way to make rubber out of milk. A great amount of serious investigation has been given to synthetic rubber, and the Germans especially used their every technical resource during the war to create artificial rubber. They did not get anywhere. No one as yet has been able to produce a rubber substitute which is one tenth as good as the worst rubber grown. But outside the scientific zone is a large zone full of cranks who have plans for making rubber out of almost any old thing. I do not know why this man decided he could make rubber out of milk. Perhaps be had eaten some cheese which reminded him of rubber, or perhaps he thought the lead was a good one in selling stock to farmers. Anyhow, he convinced a man who had some stock in our company, and this stockholder asked me to make an investigation. It was the kind of a request I could not refuse, but at the same time, if it ever got out that I had seriously considered a scheme for turning milk into rubber, I should never have heard the end of it! Every man in the rubber business would probably have presented me with a worn-out cow. "Firestone Dairy Tires," "Milk Fed Tires," "Tires from Contented Cows" flashed through my mind. I was in a hole. I told Thomas what we were up against and that he had to go along. He was almost for quitting his job—he did not want to be made a fool of, either. He explained to me that there was just as much chance of making rubber out of milk as there was of making it out of buckwheat cakes.

"You don't have to argue that with me," I told him. "This is a fool trip, but we've got to make it. This stockholder has not only been convinced but he has backed the milk man with money. He will be insulted if we turn this down without investigation. We have got to go, but also we have got to save our faces. The only thing is to sneak out and not let anybody know what we are about. We don't need a reception or a brass band."

We did sneak out—not even our families knew where we were going. We found the inventor in a couple of rooms over a village store. One room was his secret chamber; in the other, he had an ordinary churn with a lot of imposing electrical contraptions about it. We told him who we were and why we had come. He found that Thomas was a chemist.

"I won't make this rubber in front of a chemist," he said nervously. "I've got a big thing here, and no chemist is going to steal it away from me."

"That is up to you," I answered. "Mr. X, who got us here, can do what he likes with his money, but the Firestone Company is not going to invest in your process without a report from its chemist. Just say the word and we will go home."

The inventor fidgeted nervously, but he stuck to his position. We started to leave. Then he said he would make a demonstration for us if we promised not to steal his secret. We promised.

He asked us to stand where we were. Then he unlocked the door into the next room, went in, carefully closing the door after him, and in a few minutes came out with a big milk can, locked the door, and brought the can over to the churn. The can had in it what looked like milk. He poured it quickly into the churn and was as quickly closing it, when Thomas shoved his finger into the "milk" and then smelt and tasted the finger. The inventor started to bluster.

Thomas broke in on him: "You have rubber dissolved in this milk. How's that?"

It took only about five minutes to discover the whole game. The "invention" consisted of dissolving rubber and pouring the mixture into a can of milk. By manipulation in the churn the rubber came out of solution, and we had rubber from milk!

Our stockholder was all for jailing the fraud, but I held him back: neither Thomas nor I wanted to get famous through discovering that rubber could not be made out of milk. The inventor saw a great light and took himself off. That we actually did go to see rubber made out of milk has been until now our most important business secret.

As I said above, the rim business had become a part of the tire business in that no one could then sell tires to automobile manufacturers without rims to put them on. The tire companies which had their rim patents and designs pooled with the United Rim Company had their rims made by the Standard Welding Company. The pool would not do business with us, and almost before I knew it we were in more trouble about rims than we ever had been about tires. That is how I was eventually forced into the rim business. We had our own special rims, and the Standard Company made them for us. At the next automobile show, I was told that I was going to be put out of business—that I was infringing patents, and so on. Soon after that, the Standard company told me that it would have to quit making rims for me or lose all the United Rim business. I asked them to keep up the supply for sixty days until I could find someone else to make me rims. It was vital—I did not intend to be put out of either the tire or the rim business.

I found a manufacturer who had an equipment of electric welding machinery with which he was manufacturing spring wheels in a small way. He needed business, and being both an intelligent man and a good mechanic, he had little trouble in devising a way of manufacturing fine rims—better rims than I had ever had at 10 percent less than the Standard's price. He quickly got into manufacturing, but soon he received notice of infringement from the United Company. I had a two-year contract with him, but I saw that the attitude of the rim pool made depending on an outside source for my rims dangerous. The pool had a great deal of power and I had very little. My manufacturer's resources were small-he was just starting in business—and I was afraid he might have to quit. My only safe course was to go into the rim business myself. It would take several months to get my own rim plant going, and I laid my plans for starting my own business.

The first step was to get a man who knew steel and steel-making machinery. I went to I. W. Jenks, who was then general manager of the Carnegie Steel Company in Pittsburgh, and said to him:

"I am forced to go into the rim business. Nobody in our company knows anything about steel. Can you get me a first-class man, the best man you have, a man who knows all about steel, to give us a start?"

Mr. Jenks recommended a man, and we fitted up a shed beside the factory and started a man designing rim-rolling machinery. Our first rims were pretty crude. We kept on making them, although we scrapped nearly all that we made. But, finally, we learned to make good rims.

The biggest thing in business is to be working and planning ahead—planning ahead for production, for sales, for new developments in the art, for money, for sources of supply. The business of the day is, of course, highly important, for unless today's business be looked after, there will be no tomorrow's business to bother about. But unless one can see and plan for a year or two ahead, one's business will not grow evenly and naturally. It will pass through a series of emergencies, and one of those emergencies will wreck it. Emergencies will come about in any business, but they will be few and not hard to meet if the future has been mapped.

This is so self-evident that I wonder why it is so much neglected. The only danger in mapping the future lies in making the plans inflexible. No one can know exactly what will happen next month, let alone next year, but reasonable plans can always be made, and then they can be changed as circumstances require. A too rigid plan may be worse than no plan at all.

The automobile companies did not like the two dollar royalty charged by the United Rim Company, and the rim pool eventually blew up. Having started in the rim business, we found that we could make rims cheaper and better than we could buy them, and so we kept on at it, and out of it grew the rim business which forms such an important part of our enterprise.

89

The United Rim Company dropped out, but before long, another rim contender appeared and made a fight which, had it been successful, would have tied the whole rim business into a knot. The attempt of Louis H. Perlman to monopolize the demountable rim caused one of the most sensational suits in automobile history, and although its conclusion carries us well ahead of our story, it might as well be told here as elsewhere, for it marks the last attempt to bring any basic principle in the automobile industry under the control of a patent. Perlman, in 1906, filed an application in which he claimed to be the original inventor of the demountable rim, and in 1913, finally secured a patent which covered all forms of rims wedged on to the felloe—that is, which covered every form of demountable rim then being made. He filed suit against the Standard Welding Company, which was making most of the rims in the country. The Standard Company took the suit as a joke, but Perlman won in the District Court and the joke ceased to be funny. Everyone in the rim business, however, thought that his claim, would be dismissed on appeal. But in February, 1916, the United States Court of Appeals affirmed the decision of the lower court, and there was no longer anything in the nature of a joke about the proceeding. The Standard Company had to close its rim factory.

The decision gave Perlman the complete control of the whole rim business of the country, for it applied to rims to take solid tires as well as those to take pneumatics. I was in Augusta, Georgia, on a vacation when the Court of Appeals handed down its decision. I felt that there was something queer about this Perlman patent, and even though the opinion of the court did not leave me a leg to stand on, I determined to go ahead making rims and somehow to fight the patent. I knew that I was right and that I should have to win, for right, in the end, always wins. I thought Augusta was as good a place to think over the situation as any other, and so I did not break my vacation—in spite of a sheaf of telegrams to come home. One thing at a time is a pretty good rule—a rule that I never break.

When I returned from my vacation, I consulted with C. C. Linthcum, whom I have always considered the greatest patent lawyer that ever lived. He had handled my first patent case in Chicago, and I well remember that he asked a retaining fee of $500, but when I explained to him that I had only $1,000 altogether in my business, he laughed, waived the retaining fee, and prosecuted my case with as much ardour as though I had been his wealthiest client, and finally charged me only $250 for a very large amount of work.

After that, I consulted him on every patent matter, and we had a great many of them, for although I have never sued for the infringement of a patent held by my company, I have frequently been forced into patent litigation. I talked with Mr. Linthcum about the Perlman patent. He thought the Court of Appeals was wrong, and that it was more than odd to have a fellow coming out of the woods with a patent covering a whole industry after that industry had been in full operation for six or seven years. There was no record of Perlman ever having tried to sell his invention in the beginning. But, in the face of a Court of Appeals decision, Mr. Linthcum did not know any way out. He advised me to make the best deal I could.

We kept our rim plant going. I knew that some day I should get a notice to come in and settle up. But in the meantime, I should let sleeping dogs lie. I was mightily active in other directions. With Mr. Linthcum and Frederick P. Fish, who was attorney for the National Automobile Chamber of Commerce (for naturally the automobile makers were against the threatened monopoly), we began to compile Perlman's life history. W. J. Burns took charge of the job. He found the original rim which Perlman swore he made in 1906, and, scraping off the paint, discovered the stamp of the old rim association which Perlman had not taken the trouble to file out! The "original" rim had been made in 1912 and not in 1906. Then we knew we were on the trail of a fraud. Burns traced Perlman to England and found that he had been in jail there and was actually a fugitive from justice. It was about as thorough a job of investigation as I could imagine, and it was well worth the $18,000 it cost me.

We were not ready any too soon. In six months, the Perlman people went into the Federal Court in New York City—the same court that had sustained the patent in the first instance—and made application for an injunction restraining the Firestone Company from making rims that infringed their patent. I agreed to put up a bond, and so avoided an interlocutory injunction, and in sixty days we came on to trial. I was at the Waldorf Hotel the day before the trial, and some of our lawyers, being afraid that our evidence would not get in, urged me to make a settlement if I could get one at ten cents a rim royalty.

We went to trial before Judge Learned Hand. We had engaged Martin W. Littleton, because of his great trial experience, to cross-examine Perlman. Judge Hand, looking over our array of counsel, for in addition we had retained Edward Rector and Charles Neave, and seeing that Mr. Littleton was going to take charge of the trial, asked Mr. Fish rather sharply;

"Are you getting too old to try your own patent cases?"

"No, your Honour," answered Mr. Fish, "this is not a patent case—it is a criminal case."

Perlman heard this, and when he took the stand he was very nervous. He got through the direct examination by his own counsel, Melville Church—another great patent lawyer—and then he was turned over for cross-examination.

Mr. Littleton had him on the stand all day, and he answered his questions freely and cleverly. We were nearing adjournment when Mr. Littleton suddenly asked:

"Mr. Perlman, did you ever go to Europe?"

Perlman all but collapsed. "I can't remember," he stammered.

Mr. Littleton had in his hand a copy of a patent medicine advertisement that had to do with the fraud for which Perlman was arrested in England. Perlman saw the advertisement. Mr. Littleton asked:

"Were you ever in jail in England?"

"I can't remember," came the whispered answer. And that was the only answer he could give to any question.

Mr. Church arose and asked permission to withdraw from the case; of course, he had known nothing of any dishonesty.

"I will not let you withdraw," said Judge Hand. "The court will adjourn until Monday morning, and I will go on with this case at that time if I can find a way of doing it."

We never did go on. That patent is as good today as ever it was, but no one recognizes it. I do not know what became of Perlman.

Had the patent held, the public would be paying him around six million a year in royalties. To go back. We boomed along through 1906, and we boomed along through 1907, almost doubling our previous sales, when, without warning, the Knickerbocker Trust Company in New York closed and the Panic of 1907 flashed on the country. I was in New York. I telephoned the factory to close down until I found out what was going to happen. Everybody in New York was desperate; money vanished all at once, and clearing-house certificates had to take the place of currency. I had a line of $60,000 at one bank. I had never taken the full line, and I had always cleaned up once a year. At the time, I had with them only a note for $20,000. I went to see the president and asked him for more money. I was certain my line justified it. "No," he said coldly, "we will not take any more paper, and we shall expect you to reduce your present note by at least $5,000 when it falls due."

This was in August; the note was due in November. There was no use talking. I simply said, "Good-day" and left. I had particularly wanted that money to make payment on a carload of rubber that was due to arrive at Akron. I called up the consignors and told them that I should not be able to pay for the rubber when it arrived, and asked what I should do.

"Unload it and use it and pay for it when you can," was the answer. "We're all in the same boat."

When that $20,000 note became due at the bank, I did not reduce it—I paid it in full and got out of the bank.

For by then the panic was over. It had come and gone with lightning swiftness, and it left us in better condition than we ever were.

94 " I like the one you have!"

Chapter VIII
Management and Frills

The Panic of 1907 was the turning point in the automobile industry. Our sales for that year amounted to $1,600,000, which was $600,000 over the sales of the year before. We made forty-four thousand tires as against twenty-eight thousand tires. We went ahead at a rate that almost took us off our feet. In 1906, we had thought well of ourselves for having pushed our sales above the million mark; in 1910, our sales exceeded five million dollars and we made 168,000 tires. Our profits for 1909 had crossed the half million mark, but, in 1910, we made $1,394,835—that is, we much more than doubled the profits of the previous year.

This was not easy going. We were cramped for space, for, although our tires were not made entirely by hand, as in the beginning, yet hand work predominated. We had some conception of what might be done by machinery, but we were new at the business, and in addition, it was a new business. Looking back, I actually do not know how we got out our production with the facilities and the space we had. Our tires were good tires and above the average of that day, but could not be compared with the standards of the present day.

Besides, the roads of the country were not up to any average. We had no conception of the proper air pressures for tires and air pressures were not kept to any uniformity. The general practice was to put in as much pressure as the pump you had would deliver. Anyone who got four thousand miles out of a tire was doing well; now, if a consumer does not get ten or fifteen thousand miles, he does not feel he is getting full service.

Most of the work was on my shoulders. I entirely managed the finances, supervised the production, and had the direction of even much of the detail of sales. I had not learned much about managing myself. The management of one's self, which gets down to controlling one's own time and distinguishing the important from the unimportant, comes only from experience. Every man has to work out his own rules and, like all personal rules, they have to be flexible.

We were in continual need of money. We had kept our capital at $300,000 but had added to it more than eight hundred thousand dollars in surplus. Most of this surplus was in plant and equipment—in fact, far too much of it, for I like to keep a ratio of at least three to one between quick assets and current liabilities. Our working capital had in it too large a percentage of borrowed money which had to be continually replaced, and our sales were increasing at such a rate—requiring ever larger sums to finance—that I spent much of my time in the finances and arranging lines of credit with banks. We urgently needed a new factory, and, in 1910, we determined to have one. To attempt to build it out of current receipts would have been suicidal. I have never liked the fixed charge of mortgage indebtedness, and also our surplus was too large as compared with our capital stock, so we determined to increase our common stock to $3,000,000, and issued $1,000,000 in 7 percent preferred stock. I had no difficulty in disposing of this stock, most of the common being taken up by men who were already shareholders.

We thought we were financed for all time. We did not know that we had hardly begun to finance. We began work on what is now known as Plant 1 and also on the power house. Plant 1, like the financing, was to be good for all time. We worked months over the design of that plant. One of the essentials was that it could be expanded without interfering with the design, and this we arranged by providing for a series of wings which would fit right into the scheme of the building, and by adding these wings as needed, we thought that we should be good for ten or fifteen years anyhow. As a matter of fact, before the building was done, we had to begin work on some of the wings, and all of them were completed and we were starting a new building within four years. One of the objects of the new building was to cut out unnecessary trucking and handling and to make tires somewhat after the fashion that Mr. Ford was already making automobiles. To that end, I first had a big wooden model of the building constructed, and day after day we studied the model and the floor plans to see what construction would least hamper the flow of material. We were not going to be satisfied with anything less than the ideal building—and we got it. The trouble is that manufacturing operations change and the product changes, and a too neatly designed building—that is, one which is entirely special for the work in hand—may have to be scrapped when the character of the work changes. And change it must. However, our first design has proved itself adaptable to the very big changes which have come about in our methods.

But the really big problem was management. The business was already too large for me to look after alone, and yet I did not believe and never have believed in what is called "delegation." I hold that, if anything in the business is wrong, the fault is squarely with management. If the tires are not made right, if the workmen are unhappy, if the sales are not what they ought to be, the fault is not with the man who is actually doing the job, but with the men above him and the men above them, so that, finally, the fault is mine. That is my conception of business.

A company must have one head and only one, and he must be the real executive head. The board of directors can advise on policies, but it cannot run the business, and, anyway, policies never make a business successful. There is some thought that if a number of men waste a few days draughting a policy, it is the same as doing the work; a fine lot of policies are harmless enough if you can find the time to draw them up. But they are policies and nothing more. I have great respect for the written word, but no amount of writing will take the place of action. A policy is a policy, and that is all it is. And there is always the danger that a policy in effect for a long time will get into the hallowed class, and the organization will take it as inspired. A bad policy is worse than no policy at all, and policies have a way of going bad. The world changes, and policies must also change. I know of only one first-class policy. It runs:

"Use what common sense you can under the circumstances."

I said that I did not believe in delegation. Let me explain. It soon became obvious to me that if I tried to follow every detail of the business through every minute of the day, I should not have time to think and plan. That was one point. The other was that no men would be developed to run the business—they would all wait for orders. And so I began gradually to work out some method by which I could know the details—for any business is made of details—and still not be swamped by them. Success is the sum of detail. It might perhaps be pleasing to imagine one's self beyond detail and engaged only in great things. But, I as I have often observed, if one attends only to great things and lets the little things pass, the great things become little—that is, the business shrinks.

It is not possible for the chief executive to hold himself aloof from anything. This I learned from experience. I thought when I started out to build an organization and thus give my-self time to plan, that I could devise a self-acting paper or-ganization and that, by dividing up the work and delegating the responsibility, the company would run of itself. Not all at once, but gradually, I contracted the chart fever. The first step was to departmentalize the business, which is always a fine, satisfying thing to do. And, naturally, when one gets the business into departments with department heads, those heads begin to departmentalize their own departments. And just as naturally, the head of a big department has to be a vice president and imitate the president in doing nothing but di-rect. Gradually we got an organization—a real organization, second to none in its division of duties. It seems—now that it is all over—that we never faced a duty without dividing it; I did not attempt to follow the divisions and subdivisions, for that was the duty of the vice presidents, and, under the rules of the game, I was not to interfere with them. And then, inev-itably, the men began to write letters to one another. I know of no better way of fooling one's self than writing interoffice communications and asking for reports. A man can keep himself busy that way all day long and completely satisfy his conscience that he is doing something worthwhile. We wrote so many notes that the vice presidents and their assistants and their assistants often used to get a day or two behind in the reading of them, and we had to devise a bright red inter-office telegram for really urgent business!

The reports! No man will ever know how many reports came into our organization. And every one of these reports was analyzed and compared with other reports. Not one of the vice presidents could possibly read all the reports which came to him regularly by his order, but just by looking at the pile of unread reports on his desk he had the pleasant feeling that, even if he did not know what was going on, at least he had the facts before him. We erected the most elaborate sales organization that man could devise—I shall tell more about it in a later chapter—and that meant more reports and more notes and letters.

This organization did not grow all at once; it really did not reach its full bloom until 1919. But it was the logical conclusion of what I started eight years before when I began to organize. I did not think out all the marvellous turns and twists which were developed-the brain of no one man could have done that. But I was responsible, for I let the business get away from me in the easiest of all fashions—by thinking of an organization as something of itself instead of as a means of getting work done quickly and well. We were passing through a highly prosperous time, and whenever any question arose as to whether or not we were doing exactly the right thing, the increase in sales gave the answer. That is the trouble with prosperity—it hides the defects of a business. When the smash of 1920 came and half the business of the country found itself going under, we came to our senses, for we, too, as will be later told, came close to the jumping-off place. But if ever a business needed reorganization or better deorganization, it was ours.

We did just that. The charts went out the window, we abolished offices and departments, we called for all the forms that were in use. They came in by the hundreds, and with nearly every one came a note saying how essential it was. We paid no attention to the notes. We went on the principle that the form had to contain information that we could not do business without—or it went out. We cut down to the bare necessities, such as

shipping blanks, invoices, and branch reports of the most ele-
mental character. We reduced our statistical department from
thirty-five people to three-and now we can get any statistics we
want, where before we got only reams of stuff we could not understand. We cut the office force from 1,000 to 800 and found
we had left plenty of clerks to do everything that needed doing.

We now have no statements made up for purposes of record—
the test is, are they used? It is impossible for a new form of any
kind to come into existence without, not only the approval of
the higher executives, but also my approval. It takes a brave
man to suggest a new form around our office. We have only
one vice president, and he is actually the vice president—he
acts for me. Our scheme is a very simple one. It can be stated
thus:

"We are all doing this job together under the president and the
vice president; each man has his special duties, but they con-
verge upon the one point of getting the job done."

This plan of organization, which is hardly formal enough to be
called organization, works. That is the proof of it. Every man
has plenty to do and the responsible heads are so few in number that there is no opportunity to pass the buck into some other department or to jockey for favourable positions. In other
words, there is no opportunity for office politics—which is the
hardest thing to avoid in any large organization, for we are all
by nature more or less politically minded and more especially
so in the State of Ohio!

I keep my own duties from being formal. I am not in direct
charge of anything, but also I am in direct charge of everything.
The only firm rule I have is to take up one thing at a time and to
take up nothing else until my mind is free. I do not believe in
quick decisions unless in an emergency. I would rather take my
time about making up my mind, and I nearly always manage
to do so. Indeed, anything that can be decided in an instant is
something that ought not to come to me. My mail is read before it reaches me, and I see as little as I can of it, for I do not
like to write letters. In fact, I have no period for dictation, and

my letters are nearly always personal. The business letters can usually be better written by someone else. I do not write memoranda notes about to members of the organization—we have all cut that out. I telephone the man or have him come in to see me if there is anything to be discussed. All of this saves time. The writing of letters can be a great time waster. I look at the monthly letters from the branch managers and the comments on the work of the branches as made by the auditing department. All the reports first go to Mr. Thomas, the vice president, and are by him analyzed before they come to me. If the record is satisfactory, then the reports do not have to be taken up further; if it is unsatisfactory, then we go into reasons. I want to have these reports so summarized that they can be taken in at a glance. The principal reports are:

1. Comments on Factory Operations. This is a monthly report running to about ten pages, but I seldom read it, for a digest is attached which gives me all that I need to know, and this digest runs only to a single page. Here is a sample digest with the figures omitted:

101

The weight of production for June was ___ lbs., an increase of ___ % over May. June production exceeded the previous high month (April) by ___ lbs., caused chiefly by the large increase in Solids.

The labour and overhead cost per pound decreased from ___ to ___.

The weight of waste per ___ lbs. of production was ___ as compared with ___ in May and a twelve months' average of ___.

Seconds Loss amounted to $ ___, an increase of % which corresponds with the increase of ___ % weight of production.

Loss due to products scrapped increased from $ ___ to $ ___.

Reclass Loss at both Akron and Branches shows a decrease in June.

Overtime Hours show a decrease of % ___.

Coal cost for June is ___ ¢ less per ton than in May, and ___ ¢ under twelve months' average.

Benzol recovery shows improvement in June, the percentage being ___. The figures for July show considerable improvement.

Plant One Air Bag average decreased from ___ cures to ___.

Plant Two shows an increase on ___ size from ___ to ___, and on the ___ from ___ to ___.

The percentage of Seconds more than doubled on. Solids and Balloon Tubes at Plant One. Balloon Tubes at Plant Two increased ___ %.

Finished Goods Inventories at Akron and Branches decreased $ ___.

2.   A summary of sales under the heads of "Manufacturers' Net Sales," "Net Trade Sales," "Export and Miscellaneous Sales," and "Total Net Sales." This is given to me in summary for the month that has just passed and for the two months preceding it and in day-by-day detail for the month, but usually I look only at the summary.

These reports take no time at all if affairs are moving right, and I do not want to give time to reports, I want to have my time free.

Of formal meetings we have only three. The monthly meeting of the Board of Directors, the biweekly meeting of the Executive Board, made up of the officers, and the products meeting, which takes place weekly or as much oftener as may be necessary.

Of these the products meeting is the one that I most frequently attend, for in it occur the discussions vital to the business. It is composed of the superintendents of the factories, the heads of divisions, whatever laboratory men may be needed, Mr. Thomas, and myself. We review in that meeting the state and the efficiency of production and take up any improvements or new products; there can be no changes in the product without the vote of this meeting. I know of no better way to keep affairs coordinated than through such a meeting. We touch nearly everything.

I have not mentioned the financial control. By means of the summaries of the reports, my talks with the men who come in, and by occasional and unscheduled trips about the plants, I can keep a close grasp of what is going on. The financial affairs are as easily disposed of, for I find that if I continually know these items, I know pretty well what the whole business is doing:

Sales.

Profit and loss.

Plant investment.

Relation of quick assets to current liabilities.

But getting to a position where I could control the finances without having to keep them in my head was a long process. I found it necessary to have a budget and to have it for a year ahead, but my own common sense taught me that the human being is yet to be born who can make a rigid plan covering twelve months in the future without running into the danger of suddenly operating a plan instead of a business. If it were possible to plan for a year ahead, then there would be no need for judgment or management—any question that came up could be settled by referring to the plan. That is the trouble with a plan, especially a carefully considered plan. We are so likely by tacking the name "plan" on what is only a guess to give more dignity and weight to the plan than it deserves. On the other hand, without any plan at all, the necessary constructions and improvements cannot be made in the most economical fashion and, above all, the money requirements cannot be arranged for in advance.

Nothing is easier than to budget in mechanical fashion. You can start with a 10 percent increase in business, and you can fool yourself right at the outside by calling that 10 percent increase normal. There is no normal increase in business. The consumption of the country does not, reviewing all lines, regularly increase 10 percent a year. Some lines in some years increase more than that, while others increase less. But in no case does the increase come regularly year by year, and even when we have an increased consumption of, say, 10 percent in any one commodity in a single year, it by no means follows that every manufacturer of that commodity is also going to have a 10 percent Increase—his share of the increase will depend on how good he is. He may get a 50 percent increase, or, again, he may go into bankruptcy.

104

In the tire business, the limit that can be sold by all the manufacturers is fixed by the number of cars and trucks. We have accurate figures on the number in use and their classifications, because each has to be registered with the state of its domicile. Therefore, we also know where the cars and trucks are. We can learn from the production estimates of the motor companies how many new cars and trucks they expect to make and hope to sell. We do not precisely fix quotas for our various districts, but we do have a certain standard of sales in dollars per car per year, and this represents the total of what we ought to be able to do. But it is only a guess, for we may not be able to force each dealer to sell his quota, although, by careful checking and weeding—which I shall take up in a later chapter—we get rid of the dealers who consistently fall down.

But still other considerations have to enter our estimate of production. The condition of the crops will affect the farmers, although we naturally do not take the farmers as a class, for the farmers are never all broke or all flush at one time. The condition of business in the industrial districts will profoundly affect all of our sales and especially our truck-tire sales, or, then again, we may decide that our product justifies forcing sales a little, although we are not very keen about forced sales growths.

We estimate our production for a year ahead, and from this figure of production we build up our cash requirements for the year, and there we get into even greater difficulties than in estimating production, because we meet a varying factor over which we can exercise no control-rubber. We plan our extensions out of surplus already in hand—which is the only safe way, for planning extensions out of expected profits is sure to lead to trouble. We can estimate our wages and fixed charges with a high degree of accuracy, and we know the turnover on our collections, but we cannot know the amount of the collections on a given sale of tires unless we know the price of the tires. We buy rubber four months ahead and set the price of finished tires on the average of our stock and commitments. We do the best we can to forecast the price of rubber, but we never fool ourselves into holding this forecast to be anything more than a guess.

Out of it all we get a budget which will give at least our maximum cash requirements, and then our contact man, who is the assistant treasurer, visits the banks and arranges our lines. He has the formal dealings with the banks. I cannot visit all the banks, for we maintain around sixty accounts, but at least once a year, and usually oftener, I call on the larger banks, not so much to arrange anything as to get advice and, if possible, criticism. I like to know what the people who are lending us money think of us, and I like to get what help I can from their experience, which covers a great many different kinds of business, while my own experience is necessarily limited to my own affairs-at least, those are the only affairs which I can know intimately.

The budget is the general guide, but it is nothing more than that. The budget which actually controls us covers only four months ahead—that is, our rubber period. This budget is accurate; we cannot tell exactly what our sales will be, even for four months ahead, but we do know all our cash requirements for rubber—and at the present time rubber is about 60 percent of the cost of a tire. We always know just about where we are going to be in four months, and although this is not a long period, it is the longest period over which I have been able to obtain data that can be reduced to a statement which is not merely a conjecture. There is nothing wrong about guessing in business, unless you call it "estimating" and attach an undue importance to it. I want to know when I am guessing and when I am dealing with facts.

And in a period of rapid expansion, it is no easy affair to keep this balance.

108 "We have a department which does nothing but view each operation with the two controlling questions in mind: Is it necessary? Can it be simplified?"

Chapter IX
Is it Necessary? Can it be Simplified?

The first question I always ask myself when looking at any operation—whether in the shops or in the office—is this: Is it necessary?

Very often it is not necessary at all, but merely a tradition. For instance, it was a tradition that rubber had to age in the warehouse a long time before it could be used. Rubber is expensive and aging cost a lot of money—for we had to keep a deal of money in idle rubber. Everyone told me that this aging was absolutely necessary, but no one could tell me why it was necessary. I suggested that we try going ahead without aging and see what happened. We did go ahead—and nothing happened. The tires stood up just as well as they ever had, and we saved millions. Someone back in the past must have laid down the rule that rubber had to age, and everyone else had followed without question.

That is the way with a lot of things. If I do find a process or operation necessary, then I ask: Can it be simplified?

By pressing these two questions, it has come about that we are making tires with fewer men than ever we did, that we are making tires cheaper than ever we did (disregarding, of course, the cost of rubber), and that we are making them better.

We have cut our manufacturing turnover from sixty to fifteen days. We have cut our seconds to a negligible fraction, and we have so simplified processes that, whereas a few years ago we were in pressing need of space in which to build more tires, we are now, with a far larger output than then, using less than all the space we have at our command. All of this is due to: "Is it necessary?" and "Can it be simplified?"

It has not been feasible at any time to make tires exactly as we should like to make them, because the art of pneumatic tire making has been progressing so rapidly that we have had to keep our methods of production rather flexible. In the space of a comparatively few years we have changed from fabric tires to cord tires and then to the low pressure or balloon cord tires. Each of these changes has not meant an abandonment of the former type, but an addition. Then, also, we have the very important division of solid truck tires. We make only a small fraction of the styles of tires we are asked to make, and we do not go in for any freak designs, but still the number of sizes and styles is considerable. I would not say that we are at the irreducible minimum. I rather think we are not, because roads have not been standardized. Both the automobile and the tire are still so young that it would be unwise to say what is going to happen in the future in the way of design.

The ideal plan of manufacturing would be to have a complete, separate plant for each size of tire, but that we have been able to achieve only in what we call Plant No. 2, which we built for the exclusive manufacture of tires of one size—30 x 3½ inches, for light cars—by continuous process. Now that the balloon tire has been adopted, we have found it necessary to convert one half of this factory to the manufacture of the balloon size 4.40 for light cars and are now manufacturing two sizes of tires and tubes there instead of one. It is axiomatic that if a man be given one task he will learn to do it extremely well, and it is up to management so to regulate his pace that he will do neither too much nor too little. We used to hire tire builders who performed complete operations. Now we have specialists on specific operations. Above all, we have added power-not per tire produced, but per man employed. In 1914, we produced just short of 1,000,000 tires, using 1.14 horsepower per man. Now we are producing around 7,000,000 tires, using 2.2 horsepower per man, and this will increase. The difference in the amount of horsepower per man shows immediately in the weekly earnings. In 1914, these were $21.17 on an average. Now they are $34.96 on an average; and although, in 1920, the average went as high as $54, that was an inflated wage. Keeping close track, as we do, of the cost of living in Akron, we find that our present real wages are the highest we have ever paid. And they are effective wages; in the inflated period of 1920 we produced only .89 tires per employee per day. Now we are producing 3.37 tires per employee per day, which includes a very much higher percentage of large tires, and also balloon tires, and an increased production of truck and bus tires. All of which only goes to illustrate how very rapidly efficiency can be acquired through experience.

Although it does not seem possible as yet to build separate factories for each kind of tire, we do manage to make each kind of tire in a separate department, so that under the roof of Plant No. 1 we have what are, in effect, a number of separate tire factories, and we have a department which does nothing but view each operation with the two controlling questions in mind:

Is it necessary?

Can it be simplified?

Now, take something of the elements of tire construction. If a tire had no strains to withstand other than the internal air pressure, the determination of carcass design and tire performance would be a very simple matter. By exact mathematical formula we could determine the strain caused by internal pressure, and, knowing the strength of the fabric, we could find by simple division just how many plies are required. However, in the tire, there are other strains to which these plies are subjected, and these must be considered if the tire is to be safe.

Running along a smooth road, the load on a tire is distributed over a large surface of contact. When the tire is lifted by a stone, this load is carried on that area of the tire which is in contact with the stone. The strain becomes much more concentrated, and the strength of the carcass must be comparatively greater to withstand it. Because of such things, it becomes necessary to allow an unusually high factor of safety in tire construction. If all roads were smooth and had no obstructions, no nails or glass, or other objects to cut and puncture tires, no bumps to set up local strains and bruise the fabric, a tire could be designed with a factor of safety equivalent to the usual engineering values, where stresses are known ahead of time and actual limitations determined. The usual engineering factor of safety ranges between the limits of five and ten. The factor of safety means the number of times greater the actual strength of a finished structure or object is than the strength required theoretically. For example, a 5-pound weight supported by a rope capable of supporting 25 pounds before it will break, is held with a factor of safety of 25/5, or 5. In designing automobile tires, the factor of safety in number of plies and strength of fabric varies from 14 to 20. This is more than twice the average factor of safety in customary practice. That is not the whole of tire construction, but serves to show some of the principles. The design is a matter of engineering plus experience. A solid tire is moulded, but a pneumatic automobile tire is built up in rather complicated fashion, thus:

The foundation for the whole structure is a carcass composed of a number of plies of cord or square-woven fabric, solidly vulcanized together with layers of gum between.

At the extremities of the carcass section are the beads. The beads serve the purpose of holding the carcass and tire on the rim, the exact contour of the bead depending upon the particular type of rim and tire being considered.

To protect the carcass on its sides are the side walls, and on the outside at the top, to act as a wearing and tractive surface between the tire and the road, is the tread.

Between the tread and the carcass are the breaker and the cushion.

In the general construction around the bead are also located the chafers and the bead reinforcement. These consist of extra plies of fabric inserted to give strength and wear at that point. With the exception of the rim, these parts together compose the average pneumatic tire. Differences in individual tires usually consist of differences of the gauge, quality, and design of these parts. Some few tires have special features, mostly more or less fantastic, but these are the exception.

A gum tube serves to retain air within the casing and gives the tire its pneumatic qualities, while a flap protects this tube at the base of the tire around the beads. In making tires we have to consider three large factors—the "cushion," that is, the riding quality; the "mileage," or riding quantity; and the "skid," or ability to hold the road. It is easy enough to make a soft riding tire, but not so easy to make one which will endure. It is easy enough to make a tire which will give tremendous mileage, but it would not ride easily, and what the customer would save on tires he might lose on jars to his car. The balloon tire is our best approximation of all three qualities—but of that later.

It is not necessary to detail all the operations or to go into a technical description of tire making. I only want to point out some of the larger changes and improvements which have been brought about.

We began machine building in 1912, and it was something of an experiment—so much so that those tire manufacturers who had not then gone to machine building advertised their tires as handmade. The first machinery was very simple. It consisted of a rotating core on which the fabric was applied, and the principal mechanical feature had to do with the stretching of the fabric and the stitching. But on this machine one man could build about forty carcasses in an eight-hour day. It was, in a way, the beginning of the subdivision of labour, for on the machine a man built only the carcass, where before he had built nearly the whole tire. It resulted in a more uniform product.

For building tires by hand was hard work. A good man could build seven or eight medium-sized tires a day, and the last tire was fairly certain to be a second. They built the tires on a core and applied the tension by main strength. I am referring now only to the carcass of the tire. These men received from thirty to thirty-five cents an hour. Now, on the machine a man receives from eighty to eighty-five cents an hour and uses his head more than his hands.

The present machine is interesting—it is our own development. It is on the turret-head theory and is manned by four men, each of whom performs a single operation, and on it they can do a tire a minute. We have not yet reached the point where a tire can be made wholly mechanically, and I doubt whether that will ever be possible, but this is not to say that we are not striving toward that end. If, however, we were to go back to handmade tires, I doubt if three times our present floor space would be enough to hold the men required, and we could not pay as high wages and the public would have to pay more for tires. Part of our improvements have to do with saving space as well as men, for floor space is expensive.

Take the compounding, which means the mixing of the rubber with the proper pigments. We formerly had mills forty-eight inches in length. Now we use eighty four inch mills, and the machines are equipped with mechanical mixing aprons. Now one man can mix three hundred pounds more easily and with more uniformity in the same period of time that it took him to mix only seventy-five pounds.

114

Calendering the fabric is an important and expensive stage of operations. This essentially consists of forcing a thin sheet of rubber around the cords of the fabric. We used to do this on fifty-inch calenders. Now we have gone to ninety-two inches. It was thought that these calenders had to be run at a low rate of speed in fact, one could count the spokes of the moving gears. Now, omitting the technical details, we run through calenders at ten times the previous speed. As a result, we sold half of our calenders and gained double the old production-and calenders take up a great deal of space. Continuous scales for determining the amount of rubber going into the fabric took away half the human skill necessary for the operations.

We used to lay up the rubber between each milling operation for two or three days, as tradition held that the rubber got tired. That was very expensive, and also it took up a great deal of shop room. We found there was nothing in it-just as there was nothing to aging. We cut out all this waste of storing and double handling and put in conveyor systems to carry the tires through from the raw material to the finished stage. Eliminating these "rests" for the rubber also saves us millions. Tires are built up of plies cut on the bias. We had big tables a hundred feet long and forty-eight inches wide, on which the plies were cut by men with heavy knives. Two men, working hard, could make six cuts a minute. Now a machine makes forty cuts a minute. These plies used to go in what we called "books" to the tire builders. The books were long, clumsy affairs with pages of muslin so that the calendered plies would not stick together. Now the plies are spliced ready to go on the core, and we use only a few books.

Inside the bead of a tire is what is called a flap to protect the tube from the rim. This used to be built up by hand by girls, the flaps being cut to length by hand machinery. Now the flaps are slit to the proper widths, gathered on spindles, and fed through a roller. One machine does the work of from ten to fifteen girls and takes up a space three feet by fifteen feet, while before, for the same amount of work, a space of twenty feet by forty feet was required. And speaking of space, the old tire-making machine needed a space of six by ten feet. Now, with our new machines, we require not only one third less men, but two machines will go into a space of seven feet by fifteen feet.

After a tire has been made, it has to be cured or vulcanized in order to combine the rubber and the compounds in a permanent way. This used to be one of the hardest jobs in the plant. We called the curing room the "pit." The tires on a heavy iron core were bolted into moulds and set one on top of another in the heater. Only big, husky men could stay on this job, and they could not stay for long.

Now we have abolished the pit. The tires come in on a conveyor. The iron moulds are on a conveyor, and the tires are slipped into the moulds and pressure is applied by hydraulic rams. The tires are vulcanized on a conveyor and there is no lifting, bolting, or releasing of moulds.

One kind of tire is cured on an iron core, and taking the hot tire off the core is known as stripping.

The old method of stripping tires was by crowbar and main strength, and the tire was often injured. Now we have an almost human machine, with sets of steel fingers which settle down and pull the tire off. Under the old way, a strong man could strip three hundred tires in eight hours. The machine will strip fourteen hundred in the same time.

Cord tires are cured on big, stiff, heavy air bags to keep them expanded. Getting out these air bags was a stiff job. The man had to bear down with his chest and work on the air bag with a bar, going through various gymnastics. The tires were hot, and the workmen were always blistered and sore. A good man could do a tire every two minutes, but often he injured the air bag. Now, with the machine, a man can do a tire a minute, practically without any physical exertion whatsoever.

When the tires come from the heater—that is, from the vulcanizing—they have to be washed, especially the tires with the light side walls. These were washed by hand, the bad places being scraped with emery stone and rubbed with wet waste. A good man would wash two hundred and fifty tires a day. Then we invented a machine for washing. Taking just one size tire, on a ten thousand tires a day production, this machine will wash three tires a minute, with three men for two machines—a man feeding for each machine and another man taking off for both. These three men do the work formerly done by eight men. Then there is the saving in space—washing ten thousand tires a day required a space of thirty by ten feet and that only for the washing. Now, with the machine, we not only wash but dry from twenty to thirty thousand tires a day in a space of six by thirty feet, and use ten men.

A completed tire has to be wrapped in paper before it goes out to the dealer, in order that it may be delivered in clean and perfect condition to the customer. A tape of paper is wound round and round the tire. We did this by hand. The ordinary man could wrap six tires an hour, and the exceptional man ten tires an hour, but even the best hand job was a poor job. Now, we have designed a machine which does the wrapping. It requires one man for feeding, and it wraps one hundred tires an hour and every one of them perfectly.

I have touched on only a fraction of the improvements, because I do not want to be technical. They are not precisely improvements, because that word implies only a bettering of what already is. We have made improvements in plenty, but I have not bothered to mention them. I want to keep to the fundamentals of manufacturing, which get down to: Is it necessary? Can it be simplified?

Those I have found to be the guiding rules.

118   " There is no preliminary test by means of which the quality of a man's judgment may be gauged."

Chapter X
The Human Relation

In the old days, I used to pick my own men. We all knew one another. We did not need any rules, and had any one spoken to me about labour management, I might have been interested, but not as far as our place was concerned. We just worked together.

We had only 12 employees in 1902. By 1904, we had an average of 35, and then, in the next year, we took a big jump to 130, but not until 1910 did we reach 1,000. Seven years later, we passed 10,000, and in 1920 reached a peak of 19,800. That, it will be remembered, was the year in which one was fortunate if one got one half war production. In 1902, we did a business of $150,000. In 1920, we did a business of $115,000,000, but I can say with great earnestness that financing this tremendous growth was not nearly as difficult as solving the human equation, or, to be more accurate, getting something in the nature of a comprehension of the human equation. No one ever solves the labour problem. In the beginning, all of our employees were Americans—country folk from the farms of Ohio—the kind of people we knew and had been brought up with. We had tastes in common. For instance, when we tore down the old tile building and put up a three-story brick building, we held a dance, and I sent my new seven-passenger car around to get the girls. Once, on a Washington's Birthday, I took the whole office force to Cleveland to see the automobile show and have dinner. We annually had a picnic of the whole factory and office force to some nearby lake or to the old homestead at Columbiana. We gave every employee a dollar at Christmas, and when I first went to Europe, I brought back presents for the office force. Whenever the circus came to town, we quit work long enough to see the parade, and everyone had a half day off for the county fair.

We really were a big family. There were no floaters. When we could not give a man work, he went back to the farm.

Now that condition has been modified. Our company has grown so rapidly that it has been necessary to draw native labour from wide areas, making it impossible for our labour forces to remain in contact with agriculture. About one sixth of our labour is foreign born. This element has required a great deal of consideration. It has to be trained to adjust itself to our ways. At the present time, we have succeeded in getting 45 percent of our foreign born to become full-fledged American citizens and 43 percent of the balance have taken out their first naturalization papers. We have found the Negro particularly adapted to handling our raw materials. As our organization has grown, it has become impossible for me, or for any officer of the company, or for any superintendent to know more than a small portion of the employees. To meet this situation, we have taken steps to stabilize working forces by promoting thrift and the establishment of homes. At the present time 24 percent of our labour forces are property owners. Sixty-six percent are married and 6 percent are living in homes with their parents.

We have felt it our duty to bring the foreigners into some conception of American life, and that has brought in the question of paternalism. When we had only Americans, we did not have to bother about the life of our people outside of working hours, for they were perfectly competent to look after themselves and would have rightly resented any interference. With the foreigners, it is different. We did have to look after them to some extent, but we did not want to go any farther in that direction than was absolutely necessary, because we do not believe in paternalism, yet the line between downright paternalism and taking these foreigners to an American standard of living is by no means well defined. That is the labour phase.

Then there is the management phase. One is bound to have trouble with the workers unless the managers know their business, which in turn means that they know the business of the company and give more than lip service to its policies. Take this subject of men. They are more important than capital. The right kind of men can scrape along, using very little capital, until such time as they can get more—and they will get more. A good body of men can successfully make and market a poor product. Of course, they cannot do it for long, and they are not apt to try for very long, for their resource and judgment will quickly make them aware that they are wasting their time. On the other hand, men without ability can never have enough capital, they will be continually out after money, they will think that money can substitute for brains, and, of course, they will end in the bankruptcy court.

The eternal problem of business is men. Through more than twenty-five years, I have been hiring and promoting men, and I know of no formula for either hiring or promoting. And indeed, if there were a formula, it would be of little use in any position requiring the exercise of judgment. It may be possible to devise employment tests for ordinary labour which will eliminate the least fit, but even for the lowest grades of labour these tests cannot do more than determine the man's minimum fitness. They can determine what might be called his routine fitness, but when we come to the positions which require judgment, even though that judgment is to be exercised within narrow limits, the tests fall down. There is no preliminary test by means of which the quality of a man's judgment may be gauged, and even if there were, the matter of the man's whole fitness would not be determined, for there would remain the question of his compatibility.

Just because Smith capably fills a most important position with the X Company is not a guarantee that he will capably fill a similar position with my company. His personality may exactly fit the X Company and not fit mine at all. His methods of doing work may be exactly what is needed in his company but might break up mine. There is no way of testing a man in advance. One simply has to exercise one's best judgment under the circumstances and act accordingly. That is the way with everything in business; the real important matters cannot be settled by the application of rules, although a guide may be had by the application of principles. And principles, it is well to remember, are quite different from rules.

Probably, in selecting men, one turns down some of the best qualified. That is something one can never know. But I do know that if, out of every two men you pick, one turns out well, it is proper for you to compliment yourself as a picker. On the whole, I doubt if one really does pick men for important positions. The executives who are brought in full-fledged seldom make good. The men who are of the most value pick themselves, and as a rule they come along rather slowly.

Perhaps I am old-fashioned, but I have no great liking for the kind of man who can decide quickly and with apparently unerring judgment. I have hired many of these men, and always they have fallen down in an emergency. They do not seem to wear as well as the less showy men who come along slowly. But I have already, in another chapter, touched upon management and the sort of men who make good as managers. Now we are concerned with labour and its supervision.

I have never felt that the labouring man was just a human machine to be worked until he had no more work left in him and then scrapped. That is not a pleasant way of doing business, and also it is a short-sighted way of doing business, for dissatisfied men do not give results. Therefore, we gradually evolved some basic labour policies which are very simple in statement. Indeed, they are commonplace except in execution. Here they are:

1. Provide the best possible working conditions.

2. Try to pay a somewhat higher wage than anyone else pays.

3. Provide rewards and facilities over and above what any other company provides.

4. Insist that foremen treat their men as human beings.

5. Avoid the strict definition of the duties of any supervisor or foreman, in order that no man may easily pass the buck.

These are the principles we have observed from the time when we found it necessary to have principles. They seem to be right. But expanding at the rate we did, we could not hope to have the old employees put the ideas and the ideals of the company into the newcomers—there were too many of them. And so, in 1910, we began to make the labour side of the business a major affair. We had not wholly lost the feeling that we were still a big family. For events had been moving very fast, and we did not realize that, to many of these employees, we were just a company that paid wages. There and then, from the ground up, we began to build a more intimate relation—a relation which would have something more than words behind it.

Among the first steps we took was to have the labour department list the qualifications for all the jobs in the place. We have about one hundred different kinds of jobs and—intelligence aside—these require men of varied strength.

The job analysis has enabled us to place men on operations for which they are fitted, thus making them much happier. We had to train our tire builders because, soon, the supply of expert builders was far below the demand. Therefore, it became necessary to establish a department to train the tire builders.

123

Since the war, however, there has not only been a surplus of tire makers, but we have eliminated much of the hand skill and put it into the machines, so that training, while important, is not difficult. But the new man does need "breaking in"—he needs to know the one best way of doing the work and to learn how to become a part of the company. As soon as a man is taken on, he is handed a book of instructions. When he reports for his first day's work, he is made to feel at home in his new surroundings. The second day a nice, pleasant-looking fellow just happens to be passing. Finding, somehow or other, a few minutes to spare, he has a chat with the new man, explains certain points that may puzzle him, and possibly gives him a few short cuts in the daily routine. This specialized attention is continued as long as the individual requires it. If the new man is not fit for the job he was placed in, then he is shifted at the first suitable opportunity. During the probation or schooling period, a follow-up man and the foreman quietly study the new employee.

When a new employee is hired, he is turned over to the doctors and dentists for examination, the idea being to give such employee advice as to the best means of preserving his health. Results so far have been very satisfactory, as is shown by the knowledge which our employees have in reference to avoidance of colds and balanced diets. We follow up absentees and take care of them if they are sick or in need. Then, too, we try to provide work for sub-standard men. For more than fifteen years we had two deaf-mute tire builders, who managed somehow to be excellent workers. We also had a whole squad of deaf employees under a special instructor.

It is axiomatic that, to have an interested workman, he must know what he is doing. And in these days of subdivided labour it is becoming more and more difficult to have a man realize exactly the effect of his actions. That is another of our problems. For certainly everyone will admit that the man who knows what he is doing, why he is doing it, and how it should be done is a better workman than the man who goes through certain motions, day after day, without any idea as to why he does certain things in a certain manner.

124

Suppose, for instance, that a man is working in the stock preparation department or in the tread assembling room. He is told that the materials must be of such and such measurements. He does not understand why the inspector is so careful in gauging or weighing the stock. He cannot understand why the foreman is so particular regarding the exactness of this or that fabric or rubber. He does not know the reasons behind our requirements.

But if the foreman takes the workman to the department where this product is used and explains to him the reasons why everything has to be scientifically calculated to produce certain results, then the man will have a very much more intelligent idea of what he is doing, why he is doing it, and will understand why he has to be so particular as to width, thickness, length, weight, and so forth. And that is what we are trying to accomplish—to let each man discover what an important link he is in the chain of development to the finished tire. It is one of our most important developments, and in line with it we carry a number of cooperative students who are training in the Municipal University of Akron. These students work two weeks in the factory and then attend the University for two weeks, and we also maintain scholarships in the University of Akron for such men as show the ability to go farther.

This is aside from our classes for college men and for salesmen.

The classes for college men are rather an interesting development. The idea came from my son Harvey that it would be a good thing to get together each year a group of young men just as they graduated from college and put them through a course in the tire business. The thought was that thus we might build a strong body of men for the future. For although I never went to college, I am strongly in favour of collegiate and all other kinds of education, and I believe that a man who has gone through college ought to develop powers of reasoning faster than the man who has not been to college.

On the other hand, many men coming out of college have no means of going into business, and while they may have the latent power to think, they have nothing to think about. Therefore, we believe that we are doing a real service in our college work.

We started the plan some two years ago and have by now graduated about two hundred men, nearly all of whom are in our service and some of whom are most decidedly in the way of making good.

This is our plan. In our first year we sent a man to the deans and authorities of the universities and technical schools to discuss the men most likely to suit our purposes. A certain number of these men made formal application to take our course, and then we sent out a man personally to interview each applicant. We selected men and arranged to pay a monthly salary, out of which the man could board and lodge himself comfortably. This first class not only had the whole theory of tire making explained to them, but also put on overalls and were trained in all phases of production. But this we found slowed up production without giving any real results to the students. Now we have them learn about tire making through spending a day or two in each department; the repair of tires they have to learn thoroughly.

The course finished, the men decide what department they would like to go into, and into that department they go—production, accounting, credits, engineering, sales, and so on. Those selecting sales are sent out to a dealer at our expense and kept under the eye of the branch manager until they qualify to stand on their own feet.

We have several classes a year and we are able to draw from the whole country. Our scout covers the territory from Maine to California, and we have so many applicants that, in spite of rejecting more than we accept, our waiting list is very long, for we have not considered it advisable to increase the size of our classes.

Nearly all these boys have made good, and we think we are building for the future. The man in charge of this work and who does most of the instructing is a practical tire man, also experienced in sales.

This same man has charge of the classes for salesmen which have already been described in the chapters on salesmanship. We also have an apprenticeship course extending over four years for young men who want to learn to be mechanics; we have always had a waiting list for this school, and most of the graduates go into our mechanical department. And then we have English classes for foreigners and various arrangements for night school work in Akron. If any man in our employ has the ambition to gain more education and raise himself, we do everything in our power to help him.

Our educational work is, on the whole, probably the most important work we do, for the biggest thing an employer can do is to help his men to help themselves. But also I think it is part of the duty of a large industry to make its own neighbourhood a fit place to live and play in, and in that direction we have done a great deal with our clubhouse, our athletic field, and with the residential district we have built and which we call "Firestone Park."

The clubhouse was erected in 1915. It was the first industrial club in Akron and one of the best in the United States. Here employees may obtain meals of wholesome food at cost. The dining room has a capacity of six thousand meals per day. It includes a complete bakery which supplies, not only the restaurant, but also the employees' store with baked goods. The club houses the Firestone Park Branch of the Akron Public Library. The auditorium has seating capacity for two thousand. Other features of the clubhouse are the gymnasium, bowling alleys, swimming pool, barber shop, and employees' store.

A planned and equipped athletic field is located opposite the factories and occupies a space of more than ten acres. This field has two baseball diamonds, a running track, and a grandstand of steel and concrete. On the ground floor of the grandstand are storerooms where uniforms and other supplies for athletic events are kept. Here also are locker rooms, shower baths, and other equipment. Back of the stand we shall have tennis courts and an outdoor swimming pool.

The Firestone Park Land Company furnishes homes to employees on easy payment plans. This activity was begun in 1916. At that time, the population of Akron had so far exceeded the existing housing facilities that employees found it difficult to get satisfactory places to live. To meet this situation, we bought 1,000 acres southeast from the factories to be used for building homes, and named the tract "Firestone Park." The park was platted with boulevards and with proper provision for churches, and schools with playgrounds. Sewers were built; water and gas lines were installed; trees were planted; sidewalks were laid, and streets paved. The most modern system of street lighting was installed. An extension of the street railway was made into the park. It is now also served by bus lines making all parts of the park readily accessible to the downtown retail district, as well as to the plants of the company. At the present time, the park has four churches, a grade school which will house more than twelve hundred pupils, and a high school now under construction. The centre of the park is a playground with provision for baseball and tennis. More than a thousand homes have already been built and sold on the company's easy payment plan.

Speaking in a general way, it should be no part of an employer's duty to see what the employees do with their money. It is their money, and they can save it or throw it away, as they like. But there is another side—the putting of the employees into the company as stockholders so that they will have more than a wage interest. As far as the officers are concerned, I have always taken the position that their stock holdings ought to be so material that the dividends will mean more to them than their salaries. That takes them out of the class of hired men. And it is right and proper that the officers should stand or fall with the company, for what they do makes or breaks the company.

128

With the workmen it is different. No business enterprise can be wholly safe—no investment is wholly safe. Even government bonds may go by the board, but if the securities of the United States Government should become worthless, we should have so many other things to worry about that our investments would not much matter! A workman's savings ought to be in the safest medium possible. We have provided for that through a savings bank. But more important than the investment itself is the habit of saving—and it is only within the past ten years that the workman has had anything to save. Also, the workman ought to have the chance to share in the profits of industry, not only for the gain to himself, but in order to learn the functions of industry. Bearing all these points in mind, we, in 1917, started an employees' stock savings plan by which any employee had the right to buy from one to ten shares of the common stock and pay for it through deduction from his pay envelope at the rate of seventy-five cents a week a share. An employee stockholder can also at any time borrow from our stock and bond department at the bank 90 percent of what he has paid in. If he is discharged, he may have back all his money with 6 percent interest. Later, we made the purchase of two shares a condition of employment. I am informed that we are the only large company in the world in which every employee has a stock interest.

In the period of extreme depression extending from 1920 through 1922, our stock, as well as nearly all stocks, sold off far below real values, and, naturally, some of our holders wanted to sell. But hardly a man did sell; instead, they borrowed on their stock and carried out their contracts.

The Firestone Park Bank opened in September, 1916. It has more than seven thousand four hundred savings accounts. It has deposits of more than five million dollars. We also have more than eleven thousand six hundred stock-buying accounts. This savings bank was needed. For instance, when the housing conditions in Akron were so serious, we built temporary quarters for fifteen hundred labourers. The manager of the foreign department visited this colony one Saturday afternoon and succeeded in organizing and bringing to the bank during that one day $25,000 in accounts ranging from $100 to $1,500. Several years ago a man was seriously injured in our steel plant and was told that an ambulance had been called and that he would have to go to the hospital. He thought he was going to die, so he called his foreman and asked him to take his belt and keep it for him, and if he died, to send it to his family in Austria. We found in this belt $1,800. The man lived, and when he came back his foreman took him to the bank and explained to him thoroughly the advantages of depositing his money in the bank. The money is there now, and the account is increasing. A very important service the bank renders to our employees is in its Trust Department. Here it helps them in making wills and acts as executor in settling estates.

We have found a suggestion system is of very great help, and the employees are constantly on the watch for new improvements, not only for the reward but also for the pride of having made the suggestions.

"When you write us your suggestion, make perfectly sure in your own mind that it embodies an improvement upon the

129

existing method, machine, raw material, or other item. Then, if you feel satisfied on this point, ask yourself further questions:

1. "Will more work be produced?

2. "Will better work be produced?

3. "Will quality be sacrificed for quantity?

4. "Will the proposed change pay for itself?

5. "Will working conditions be improved?

6. "If it were your plant and your money, would you make the change?

"If your answers to these questions are satisfactory, your suggestion is worth submitting. If you cannot answer these questions affirmatively, think further, analyze your suggestion, determine what is lacking, and be reasonably certain when you submit a suggestion that it is going to be adopted.

"Let us take two concrete examples, and endeavour to see why in one case only a small award is given and in another a large award is given.

1. "A suggestion that won a large award—a new tension device for wire braiding machine. This suggestion, while it did not involve nearly as great a saving as certain others, still brought a large award. It was one of comparatively few cases in which an idea was developed to a point where it was ready for commercial use. In this instance, not a little trouble had been encountered, since parts of the old device sometimes broke and fell into the gears of the machine, causing considerable damage. However, by analyzing the defects of the device which had been used and eliminating them in the development of the new one, a far superior tension from the viewpoint of mechanical perfection, as well as of appearances, was obtained.

2. "A suggestion that won a small award—clutches for belt conveyors driven from line shaft. At present, certain belt conveyors are driven direct from line shafting, and although only one of three or four machines may be in operation, the conveyor belts of all the machines are running.

It is proposed that clutches be installed, so that when a machine is not in operation the conveyor drive can be disengaged. Upon investigation and analysis, we find that the conveyor belt is worth perhaps thirty dollars, and, as it moves slowly, the wear and tear on the belt and pulleys on which the belt rides is very slight. The power loss is also negligible. The installation of a suitable clutch would cost from two to three times the value of the belt, and from the stand point of depreciation it would take several years to pay for the installation. Moreover, the maintenance cost of the clutches would perhaps be more than the present maintenance cost of the belts. And yet, not withstanding these facts, the suggestion has merit. In fact, it was adopted, but it received only a small award, for a different device, which will fill the requirements more economically, will be installed for disengaging the drive."

131

We have no formal organization. We do not believe in shop committees or in any form of self-government in the shops. But we do believe in being fair, and when a dispute of any kind arises, we take the position that the workman is right and proceed on that basis. I find it the best basis.

132 "That is what we are always
after—a permanent relationship."

Chapter XI
Some Things We Have Learned about Selling

I was brought up as a salesman. I think that I still am a sales-man—perhaps that is the reason why I know enough about selling to realize how easy it is to overdevelop the sales side of any business—to put money into sales expense that ought to be either in the quality of the product or taken off the price to the consumer.

There is a great waste in selling and especially in "hurrah" sell-ing with conventions, campaigns, contests, and all the odds and ends of high-pressure stuff that have been devised. I have tried all of it and I know. The place to start selling is in the factory, and if the articles we make are not good enough con-sistently to be sold to the public without any hypnotic pro-cesses, then they are not good enough to sell at all. There are times when extra sales pressure is useful—say, to clear out big inventories—but I should never think of putting on a sales campaign just to stimulate the salesmen. If the salesmen are not doing their work, then that is the fault either of their man-agers or of the product—or of both. The fundamental faults of management and manufacturing are only made the worse by giving artificial sales aid to the distributors or by shifting the blame for bad conditions to them.

133

Our business cannot afford to go ahead in a series of sales spurts—it makes manufacturing too expensive. The kind of selling that really helps in the long run is the steady sort that turns in orders week in and week out in a gradually increas-ing volume. And so all our efforts today are in the direction of steadiness. We want our sales to increase year by year some-what faster than the increase in the registration of motor cars. That, we have found, is the cheapest and most profitable way to do business. It does not pay to try to get the business all at once. In the first place, you can't get it, so a good deal of your money is thrown away. In the second place, if you did get it, the factory could not handle it. And in the third place, if you did get it, you could not hold it. A company that gets business too quickly acts just about as a boy does who gets money too quickly.

Automobile tires are today a commodity—even more so than leather shoes, for, although there are fashions in tires, these fashions are not now fantastic. A passenger automobile is a utility as much as a truck, and no one wants a tire just for looks. A tire has to be sold for what it will do, and no amount of enthusiasm in the sales force will make up for bad manufacturing.

So the way to advertise and sell tires is, to my way of thinking, the way to sell any commodity—that is, on service to the buyer. The job of the salesman is to find out the exact requirements of the prospect and sell to him the tire that will best fulfil those requirements; and the way to make the sale is to know tires so thoroughly that you can explain to the prospect just why you can give him a brimming dollar's worth of service.

No frills are necessary in this kind of selling, and consequently, no frills are necessary in the advertising, dealers' helps, and so on, that are designed to make the selling easier. Selling is first a matter of having something to sell, then of finding whom to sell to, and, finally, of finding real reasons why this prospect should buy.

But it took us some time to find out that frills in selling are only an added expense. We were all right in the beginning—we did not have money enough to do other than sell. But then, later, as we grew and began to make money, we went in for more elaborate methods, until, eventually, the methods got the better of the selling. Then I called a halt on it all, chucked the methods, and went back to first principles.

This is a record of a number of mistakes. We learned lot from them. So may someone else.

We are wholesalers. Our business has always been divided into the two broad classes of manufacturers' sales and trade sales—the first being to the manufacturers of vehicles who sell our tires as part of their original equipment, and the second to distributors and dealers. We have never sold automobile tires directly to the consumer, and have no intention of going into the retail business. For a large business such as ours, the matter of retailing would add too many complications. The individual independent dealer will always fill a necessary need and have an important place in the distribution system of a national manufacturer.

In our early days of solid tires, we sold directly to retailers—mostly to carriage dealers and wheelwrights. As our business became larger and worked gradually over into automobile tires, we began to establish distributors, giving to each distributor an exclusive territory. We did not have the capital to establish branches, except in three of the largest cities of the country, and even if we had had the capital, there was hardly enough tire business in other territories to support branches.

A deal is to be said both for and against giving exclusive territory, and I do not believe that the question can be decided abstractly—it gets down to cases. The advantage of exclusive territory is that whoever has the territory may be held responsible for the sales—or the lack of them. The disadvantage is that the manufacturer is tied down in his sales by the ability and ambition of the man who has the territory. In an ideal business world, one would give exclusive territory to the man best fitted for that territory, but, unfortunately, things do not work out so neatly. Almost everyone sees that it pays to sell a lot of goods, but not nearly so many see that no one sells a lot of goods who does not work hard. And hard work is, unfortunately, not a universal habit.

A small concern with insufficient capital must depend on jobbers for distribution, and there is really no better way to distribute, if the jobbers know their business. It relieves the manufacturer of a mass of selling detail. I had to give exclusive territory in order to get good distributors. Twenty-five years ago, a jobber took on a new line as a favour, and he had to be catered to and everything made just right to suit him. If I were a jobber, I should not want exclusive territory. I should want to have plenty of competition to keep me on my toes. It does a salesman good every once in a while to have a big order taken right from under his nose. When this happens in exclusive territory, the salesman who did not make the sale at once writes an essay on the injustice of the proceeding. But if the territory be not exclusive, then he can only reflect on what a poor salesman he is—which is a very profitable reflection for anyone to make now and again.

As we grew larger, we helped our distributors wherever they seemed to need help. We dealt with each distributor as an individual and on the facts. We did not consign our goods, as I never believed in consigned stock. If a distributor were deficient in salesmanship, we did our best to help him overcome this deficiency. We furnished a few signs and placards and some newspaper advertising. In the early days, I established and knew practically all our distributors myself and visited them as often as I could, and tried to build them up so that they would eventually be an integral part of our business-except that they would run on their own capital and keep their own profits. The plans worked very well, and they would have continued to work if only these distributors could have seen what I saw in the future of the tire industry. But only a few were willing to stake all they had on selling tires. The automobile industry was not generally looked on as a substantial means of earning a livelihood. It was still something of a "game." We tried to organize our distributors. We had them in for conventions, and while many of them were first class, others did not get what we thought they ought to get out of their territory.

Therefore, in 1913, we decided gradually to eliminate distributors and set up branches of our own. We did not make any sweeping changes. We simply did not renew the contracts of such distributors as were not up to the mark. Through experience we had learned that a man of moderate ability and energy could sell a certain minimum volume a year for every car registered in his territory, and we adopted that figure as the minimum which would satisfy us. When a distributor's contract came up for renewal, we judged him on his sales per car and not on his total business. If a man had done $300,000 gross, he might consider himself a pretty clever fellow, but if he had 150,000 cars in his territory, we could not agree with him, for his average per car was too low, and his contract would not be renewed. We did not disturb any distributor who kept up a good selling average per car, and we still have a couple of distributors. It would not be fair to disturb them, because they have always thoroughly worked their territories and kept up their averages.

We find the branch method the most satisfactory because now the selling of tires is on a scientific basis and we must have expert tire men in our employ all over the country, seeing that the proper kind of tires is being sold and that the proper kind of service is being given. No matter how well we may make a tire and how perfectly it may be built for a particular use, we can lose a great deal of reputation on that tire if it be put into a service for which it was not designed. We established about twenty branches and put in branch managers selected from among the distributors or from men whom we thought well of at Akron. We had to throw them in to sink or swim, because we had not in the beginning any organization for close supervision. Eventually, we developed too much supervising—but that I shall tell about later.

We paid these branch managers salaries but not commissions. We have never been fond of the purely commission basis, because many men are short-sighted and they will neglect service and the steady customer of the future for the immediate customer on whom they can earn a commission. We give to each man the opportunity to progress to a higher salary and to become a large stockholder in the company. In this way, we can weld men into the organization and build up their strength and ours in a fashion which is not possible where an employee's sole interest in his company is what he gets out of it.

The branch organizations do not touch manufacturers' sales and neither do they sell directly to consumers. Their selling is to dealers and their business it is to see that the dealers are selling to the best advantage.

Our great sales ambition, as we came to have national distribution, was to hold a sales convention. I suppose every young company has that ambition—to have a big get-together with a lot of speeches and badges and banners and flags and a dinner. We wanted a good outing all to ourselves where we could tell ourselves how splendid we were. The convention is an established American institution, and a company can hardly hold up its head in commercial society until it has had a convention.

At the time of our first convention, we could not afford to spend the money, but also we thought we could not afford not to have a convention, else our men in the field might think we were not worth working for. And then, too, we had the sound idea that those who sold our goods ought to know how they were made. Our error was in believing that the best way to show them was through a convention.

We had our convention. Twenty men came—paying their own expenses. As conventions go, it was successful. We had the distributors and salesmen out at the old plant and explained exactly how tires were made—which did not take very long, for at that time there was not much to say about the making of tires. I talked. All the department heads talked. Everybody talked. We did this for several days and wound up with a dinner at the Portage Country Club, this being the first of our annual dinners.

That convention was useful. Everyone got to know everyone else, and it was the first time that most of the distributors had seen our plant or how tires were made. It was not much of a plant to look at, but still, it was the best we had, and we were making good tires.

The convention was in every way so helpful that we fell into the natural error of believing that all conventions would be helpful and that we ought to have one every year. We did not miss a year, and it became our aim to have our entire field organization in Akron at least once in every twelve months. We had the branch managers in at one convention, the office managers at another, the service men at another, and the credit men at still another. Some years we had everybody in at once. Here, quoting from one of our early announcements, is how we felt about these conferences:

"Besides attending the general sessions addressed by company executives, branch managers, and salesmen, every representative will spend hours in the factory studying, in a practical way, the manufacture of Firestone tires. He will actually see our experts building into Firestones the 'extras' you have been reading and hearing about; that extra layer of fabric in the five inch tire; the extra ply in the three-inch; the extra coating of pure gum between the plies, etc. He will see the 'inside' reasons why 50 percent more Firestone dealers were added last year, and why our output was increased 78 percent.

"He will see five great buildings under construction to provide over seven acres of additional floor space which will increase our output of pneumatic tires from seventyfive hundred to twelve thousand a day. This increase of forty-five hundred tires per day is larger than the output of the original new Firestone plant erected on its present site four years ago.

"He will rub shoulders with hundreds of men whose interests are kin to his, and from them he will reap a great harvest of valuable and helpful information which he will use to the advantage of customers in his territory.

"These days of conference and study represent a large investment, but it produces adequate dividends in better service for tire users the world over. It means a greater, more alert, better informed Firestone organization, and that insures satisfied customers. And there you have the vital reason for it all, because—satisfied customers constitute the corner stone of this business."

Our conventions gradually became more and more elaborate. We spent a lot of money on convention booklets and had photographers snapshotting everyone. We always had plenty of enthusiasm, and, of course, each convention was the greatest convention we ever had—I regularly said so, and every other speaker regularly said so, and we convinced ourselves it was all true. We kept this up until the war, each convention being more expensive than its predecessor.

We no longer have regular conventions. It is true that the men in the field do get acquainted with one another and with the officers of the company, but it is not of the highest importance that the men in the field should be acquainted with one another, and they do not, through a convention, get intimately acquainted with the officers of the company—there is too much hubbub and artificial enthusiasm for the men to know the officers or for the officers to know the men. And also, the men do not, because of the convention excitement, really learn much about the product. Therefore, the real aims of the convention are not attained, it becomes more of a social than a business affair, and is a waste of money.

Not only is the waste of money direct in the cost of the convention, but a much larger waste is indirect through withdrawing for a week or ten days all the responsible selling men from the field. It is said that the extra sales stimulus which the men receive at the convention more than makes up for the time lost. This I have not found to be true. But if it were true, it would be an additional reason for not having a convention because, as I said before, selling in spurts does not pay.

We still have conventions now and again, but they are strictly business conventions with a very definite purpose in mind that has nothing to do with pep or ginger or sales stimulus. If we inaugurate a considerable change in manufacturing or in fundamental policy that has to be communicated to the whole force at once and cannot well be done by letter, then we have a convention. But we have only a few meetings where everyone is expected to be present, and their purpose is largely social. The real work of the convention is done in groups of ten or twenty men who are given what amounts to class instruction by an executive.

We get our personal contact more effectively by having the branch managers and many of the dealers come to Akron from time to time and treating them as guests. They can see what the plant is really like. They can see what we are really like, and thus get on a solid, permanent basis. That is what we are always after—a permanent relationship.

And that is why we do not care for sales contests or high-pressure selling. We have tried most of the approved devices for stimulating sales. For several years we set up quotas. If the end of the month were near and a salesman were below his quota, it was natural for him to go to a dealer that he knew well and say:

"Help me out with an order to make my quota."

That is not selling—that is asking for alms. A dealer with a charitable bent of mind will order to help the agent, which is no reason at all for ordering. We have had sales contests with prizes and bonuses, and these, too, were successful, in that they produced results, but the results were not permanent. When a sales contest closed, the salesmen took things easy for a week or two, and we would have a sharp drop in sales. We did not gain any permanent advantage by the contests and we did have the disadvantage of forcing irregular production on the factory as well as overstocking dealers and leading them into financial trouble. Above all, too much conventioning and too much sales stimulation do not serve to build self-reliant men. Instead, they build a class which thinks it cannot do anything without support from the outside. A salesman accustomed to living on a sales stimulant becomes an addict, and he is no good without his drug.

In dealers' helps we learned somewhat the same lesson. A dealer will make more sales if he is given some advertising assistance from headquarters. He is commonly not equipped to get out good sales letters or booklets, and even if he were so equipped, the work could be done much more cheaply from the central office. In the early days, we helped our dealers according to the circumstances of the case, with a general idea that it was good business to go fifty-fifty on almost anything that the dealer wanted—that it was more important to have the dealer feel we were with him than to pass on the merits of what he might want to do. If a dealer thought that only road signs stood between him and tremendous success, we would give him road signs. We would give him anything within reason which he held to be needful for his success. The policy worked. We had to make a few rules about kinds of advertising that we would not go into, but, on the whole, the dealers were reasonable, and even if many of the things they asked for and got did not help them, they at least thought they had been helped and in consequence worked all the better.

But then we got into the game ourselves. We started deciding what the dealers ought to have. We passed from signs and newspaper advertising and cuts furnished free or at cost to more "effective" advertising. We got out blotters and buttons. Our advertising department devised what it called a "six-cylinder" combination, which was a leather portfolio designed to carry our full line of dealers' helps. The salesman was supposed never to be without this portfolio—to exhibit it to every dealer he called on. I have a photograph before me of a model salesman exhibiting his portfolio to a dealer and demonstrating to him in a clear, forceful, and definite way that "one-cylinder" plugging away does but little good—that he must make use of our "six-cylinder" combination in order to get maximum benefit.

"It furnishes an entree to a difficult prospect," so we said. "It strengthens the tie between salesman and dealer because it helps the dealer build a permanent and successful business. Firestone is thus moved still farther away from the class of 'price competition' and sells quality with cooperative assistance thrown in."

That was fairly strong going. But we went farther and higher. In 1918, we reached our greatest height by establishing a regular magazine on which we prided ourselves mightily.

It was not a house organ. It was a general magazine. We paid up to a thousand dollars to well-known artists for cover designs. We bought short stories and articles from the best writers in the country. The only advertising was on the inside cover pages, where we told about our tires, and on the back cover, which carried the local dealer's advertisement. Otherwise, it was a general magazine and was intended to be received and read as such. It was subtle. But just how subtle, we did not realize until afterward.

We called the magazine Milestones, and while it cost us anywhere from ten to twenty cents a copy to produce, we sold it to dealers for distribution at five cents a copy. They simply grabbed for it. Some dealers bought for every car owner in their territory. Within two months we were up to a circulation of a million copies. It was the finest bit of advertising we ever put out, for, as I said, it was subtle—so subtle that as advertising it was worth to us exactly nothing.

The salesmen were charged with selling these dealers' helps— the responsibility was theirs to see that every dealer bought the necessary help to move his tires. I found our salespeople congratulating themselves on the amount of advertising they sold. I began to see salesmen's reports like this:

Fifty Milestones

One thousand blotters

Five hundred buttons

Ten tires.

Looking through the accounting department, I noticed a new division of clerks that I had never seen before. I asked what they were doing.

"Billing advertising," came the reply.

That set me to thinking. I began to ask myself:

"Are we in the business of selling tires or are we publishers and sellers of advertising?"

There was only one answer, so I wiped out Milestones and the whole advertising billing department and issued orders that thereafter our salesmen were to sell tires and nothing else.

Now we help dealers more effectively than ever we did in the heyday of our dealers' helps. We help them with their local advertising, with whatever signs are necessary, and we send out sales letters to the lists they furnish us, but we never forget that we are selling tires and not advertising.

We had big sales manuals. There was a notion that the elaborate sales manual somehow impressed the dealer. They were expensive to get out and clumsy to handle. We found that they did not impress the dealer. Now we have a small loose-leaf book.

We tried all the frills, but I have not yet told about the truly marvellous sales organization that we erected and which was, until I smashed it, the pride of my heart. Of this I shall tell in the next chapter.

All these frills of selling had nothing at all to do with selling. In the beginning, we actually sold tires, but then the great production of automobiles brought a demand for tires exceeding the supply. We thought we were selling to the public. Actually, the public was buying from us in an ever-increasing volume, because we were making good tires. Our selling efforts had nothing to do with selling, but they were amusing and kept a lot of people occupied.

No end of sales reputations are established by salesmen taking the credit for the public resolutely refusing to be deterred from buying. All of which we found out before any great harm had been done.

146   " A trained man who goes into the field
with confidence and a knowledge of
his goods can do well almost from
the start."

Chapter XII
Taking the Bunk out of Sales

It was in 1919, when the boom started, that we reached our stride in sales organization. We had been organizing rather freely whenever we had the time, but when our sales organization was laid out in chart form, it did not look pretty. It lacked the proper number of subdivisions, and it did not have nearly enough managers. So some of our best minds really got down to organizing.

I do not know where this organization bug came from, but, like the flu, it hit nearly everyone in the country. I am free to confess what it did to us, for it is over with, and we are immune. I think many other confessions might be added to mine, for I notice that most companies are not so perfectly organized as they were just after the war. The trouble is that, nowadays, one has to work, and having an absolutely perfect organization on the premises does interfere with work. In 1920, in common with most other manufacturers, we did not have to sell, as I said in the last chapter. However, we imagined that we were selling; for the constantly rising prices disturbed our old comparisons. We, and everyone else, had always figured our product in dollars, and with orders coming in by wire instead of by mail, and with the dollar figures of sales beginning to look like the war debt, it is no wonder that we lost our sense of proportion. And also it is no wonder that we fell in with all the ingenious notions for sales organization.

Every change we made in sales methods brought results—and proved the new method. We did not know that we would have shown as startling an increase had we abolished our whole sales force, closed all our branches and dealers, and just sent out our tires in freight cars to be thrown off on sidings and taken away by clamouring buyers. Many of us imagined what was happening, but our pride would not let us admit the true condition, and hence the sales department had the leisure to devise fancy trappings for itself. In ordinary times, one has to get along with things far short of the ideal, but in those days we had to have absolute perfection. That was the post-war cry everywhere.

I never did catch up with the complete organization of our sales. But it was something in this fashion. First, we had a sales manager, and under him two assistant sales managers—one for trade and the other for manufacturers' sales. I kept my hand on manufacturers' sales, so it never got really organized. But the trade sales crowd grew amazingly. The first step was to divide the trade sales into East and West, to which later was added South. Each of these divisions was a complete unit at Akron—each had a sales manager, a truck-tire manager, a pneumatic-tire manager, and an accessory manager. Each of these managers had an assistant or two, and each division a separate credit, billing, and accounting department. We also had an export department with a complete set of managers. All this was not in the field, but at Akron. It will take me some time to reach the people who were supposed to sell to the dealers. These Akron organizations compared and competed with one another, and I shudder to think of the clerical wages and good white paper that was wasted by them in showing in their several ways how good they were.

The branches had been getting along with a branch manager and an office manager. That was all wrong, and so each branch developed a branch manager, a truck-tire manager, a pneumatic-tire manager, an accessory manager, and a credit manager, all of whom had assistants. Somewhere down the line were the salesmen, who under all this supervision were supposed to sell to the dealers.

But even this supervision soon became inadequate, and some genius divided the country into five zones—on top of the branches—and each zone had an office managerial staff and a number of divisional men to go about among the branches and see that all was well. In a very short time, our sales force grew to around one thousand.

I shall never know what our sales overhead was, for, before the organization was quite perfect, we ran into the troubles of 1920, which will be told of in a later chapter. Then I was more interested in getting down to business than in finding the cost of our indiscretions. And how we did cut!

The advertising department had 105 people. We cut the force to a manager, an assistant, and about five clerks and stenographers. We wiped out the whole scheme of divisions and sections, and I became sales manager, with the branches directly under me. Their accounting and credit divisions were abolished, and their accounts cleared through the general accounting of the company. We reduced each branch to a sales manager and an office manager, and the sales manager was expected to be out in the field selling. The whole swivel-chair squad had the choice of getting out as salesmen or getting out altogether.

We went over every part of that sales organization, asking: "Can we get along without this job?" In 1921 we cut our sales force 75 percent over the peak of 1920. What is more important, we started it to selling. The pressure was intense, for salary cuts came for those who remained. Only the men stuck who could stand the gaff, and these were the only men we wanted.

Now our sales are on a sensible basis and we get results. We still make mistakes and we expect to go on making mistakes as long as we remain human beings, but we are all so close to affairs that a mistake does not get far. If a mistake be made, it is our mistake and it does not help anyone to put in time hiding it. A fair part of the time of the big, complex organization is spent in steering the effects of mistakes into other departments, and instead of an error being corrected, it is kept in the air. Our present system is not a system at all. It is direct, personal, day-by-day contact. Each month every branch manager sends me, on one small sheet of paper, a complete picture of the operations of that branch for the preceding month as to sales, collections, and standing of each salesman in sales per car and expense to sales. He also writes me a letter with this report, giving his own version of the operations of his branch for the preceding month and how he hopes to serve his trade better the following month. In this way, I get a complete history of the business in every section of the country. I pass this on to my assistant with any suggestions I have to make, and often write letters to the branches to keep in personal contact with the business and tell them of any good ideas and put into effect by certain branches.

Here are extracts from some of the letters, and they also show something of the methods:

"As you are aware, it has been our desire to eliminate as much of the detail of your office work as possible and to simplify the operations.

"The first request we will make is to have you send us a map or maps outlining with a blue pencil each salesman's territory and number each territory in alphabetical order starting with A and give us the name of each salesman corresponding to the letter of that salesman.

"We want you to discontinue keeping a daily or weekly record of your sales with the exception of your daily sales memorandum. When we receive copies of all invoices we will analyze each invoice and divide it into the classes of products. We will take from your daily sales memorandum amount of orders you receive and orders sent in by the salesmen and send you a complete analysis of your salesmen and your branches, which will include salesmen's expenses, by the 15th or 20th of the month following. This with the daily sales memorandum of total orders received each week from each salesman, and the total billings of your branch, will not give you the total billings in each territory, but you will have the total billings from your branch which will be sufficient to guide you during the month as to the operations of your branch, when at the end of the month you will have a complete analysis of each territory as described above. As stated, we ask you to discard all sales records except the ones we have asked you to keep."

This concerns what selling is:

"I am continually advising the organization not to compare present-day business with our past records—although it is a natural thing to do. We are doing much better business than we did last year. But to do a better business than we did last year really is not much credit to us. We must compare what we are doing to-day with our opportunities of today."

Getting the branch managers away from their paperwork was not easy:

"It seems exceedingly difficult to get our branch organization to 'think.' Of course, it is difficult for all of us to think hard enough and long enough to get a clear picture of the problems before us. Most of us go only part of the way, too many times, and some of us never get a clear vision or finish our problem, and that means failure, no matter how good our intentions are or what energy we exert.

"I refer particularly to the simple routine of the management of your business. If you cannot get your office and branch working smoothly and without too much friction, it is plainly evident that you cannot handle your salesmen, customers, and accounts successfully or to any degree of efficiency, if the mental machinery of your branch is not working right.

"I know the home office will plead guilty of giving you every variety of detail known to accounting in the past few years. But I feel that they are now simplifying it and have a clearer vision of your problems and the important things you should know about your branch, and are giving you an opportunity to get a grasp in a simple way so you can get a clear vision.

"In the letter I sent to you on June 15th we enclosed a daily sales memorandum. I don't know how a form could be made up more simply or how a letter could explain more fully what this memorandum was intended for and how to use it. If there could be any question, it would be in the request that you stop all other statistics that you are compiling on your own accord.

And I would say further, do not insert the salesman's salary. All we want in the expense column is the salesman's expenses, how much money he spent that week, either railroad, auto, or any other expense. (The salary you can get at any time.) I cannot imagine any of our branches complicating this simple form and instructions and yet they have. One of them writes:

"'Your Daily Sales Memorandum, as outlined in letter, will not give a true picture of the daily activities by salesman, and if we understand it correctly, is not workable.

"'It is a simple matter to enter each salesman's daily orders as they come in from blue copy, figured in dollars and cents. All other orders, however, taken by phone or via mail, are not figured until ready for billing, and if we are to stop and figure all these as they come in, it is going to make quite a delay before they reach the Shipping Room.'

"Another branch says:

"'On Monday this report will show orders which our salesmen have taken on Friday and Saturday of the past week, therefore will not at any time agree with what he has actually sold during the week, neither will it agree with his actual billing. In fact, the billing does not show the true sales as, at the present time, with the small force, the billing is at times a day or two behind.'

"You can see from the above that these two branches are trying to make hard work and complicate this simple form. I hope none of the other branches are. It has occurred to me that it might be confusing, as the month does not always end on Saturday. But if you will just record your daily operations, and if you desire to stop at the end of the month, start a new sheet at the first of the next month, there will be no confusion. Or, you can close it at the end of each week without any reference to the date of the month. I think the former would be the better way. All you want in this report is a correct statement of your daily operations, and then, at a glance, you can see from which salesmen you received orders, what the total orders, total billings, and total receipts were for the day. You can see if you are carrying too many orders without being shipped or billed. It gives you your branch operations quickly and is not a record that serves as beautiful history."

This was written in 1922 during the bleakest period of the depression:

"I have recently spent some time at the branches, this giving me an opportunity to get first-hand information from the branch managers and salesmen. The two outstanding points on which many men seemed to fail and which are essential to success were these:

1. "Knowledge of product.

2. "Knowledge of organization to the end of selling the product.

"However, the two things that I have mentioned are vital and necessary to bring up the standard of our sales organization. How are you going to accomplish it for yourself? I can tell you, but the method is so simple that you will not realize the sacrifices you must make and the difficulties you will encounter to prepare yourself that you may know the value of our product by comparison with other tire values, and that you may direct each day's energy and concentrate on each problem to a final conclusion, and give a decision on that subject or problem at hand.

153

"You are not going to get this fundamental foundation for your success or the success of your salesmen by any long dissertation in book or letter, or oratorical accomplishment from an Akron representative—you are only going to get it from your own concentrated thought and energy. I mean by that, that you will not get it so that you can effectively pass it on to your salesmen and dealers.

"As I said, the formula is so simple and yet so difficult that any suggestion I might make would not be effective for everyone. However, this might be a start for you to get a more thorough knowledge of our product—purchase your leading competitor's fabric and cord tire (and if you feel you can accomplish results, this is your authority to purchase these tires), take them into your branch, cut them up and cut up our fabric and cord tires, call in some reliable repair man and analyze them for yourself. You can get from the laboratory at Akron the exact sizes of every tire, the rubber volume, the quality of the fabric, and the details of the tires (you probably have this now in your files). However, don't let that prevent you from asking Akron for what you want.

"The other point is a simple suggestion, that you organize your daily work and concentrate your energies on each problem and see it through to the final finish. When you go to call on a customer, know just what you want to accomplish and stay until you finish it, and impress this upon your salesmen.

"I wrote a letter to each of your salesmen and have had a number of replies. Most of them show thought and are inspiring letters. I hope to have a letter from each salesman, as we are making it a start of a file for each salesman for his sales, expense, and field reviews. We are planning to get out a new General Report to take the place of the field review. We will want each salesman to make a General Report once a week to the branch and send a copy here. I hope this report will be free expression of the salesman's thoughts on the conditions in his territory and suggestions for improvements. What I want is to have you and your salesmen assume the responsibility for raising the standard and increasing the business in your own territory."

A letter to salesmen written during the same period:

"I have a keen realization of your difficulties and have given a great deal of thought to your problems. As a whole, they may seem very large, but by taking each one separately and analyzing it carefully, you will find them surprisingly easy of solution. Overcome the habit of allowing small difficulties to become exaggerated in your mind by thinking out clear and convincing arguments against them.

"The greatest difficulty everyone faces today is to keep from becoming discouraged and disappointed at conditions. Sympathizing with ourselves over personal disappointments and the business situation only weakens our courage to face our problems and lessens our determination to give a full measure of service. Then we begin to question whether we are engaged in the right business.

"This I think is particularly true of the tire business. It has been very prosperous, and all of us had wonderful visions of the future. But the losses sustained and the personal economies we have been forced to make have been irritating and discouraging to many. Everyone looked forward to easy prosperity. When conditions changed, many were unable to adjust themselves and have spent much time and energy looking for a line of activity that would not require any hardship and sacrifice...

"I realize that we have been the leaders in reducing prices to the consumer. This policy is based upon fundamentally good business, not only for ourselves, but for all dealers who want a permanent and profitable business. However, in bringing down prices, it is absolutely necessary that we prove to dealers and consumers alike that our quality has not only been maintained but improved. The public is very apt to associate lowered prices with cheapness. In the public mind the word "cheap" does not imply quality or value. The same thought is apt to creep into our organization in the reduction of salaries and expenses. So we must guard against it constantly. It takes character and courage to reduce our living expenses and at the same time keep up appearances and be happy. But that is our job today.'

This went to both managers and salesmen:

"On Wednesday evening I attended the Factory Suggestion Board dinner given in honour of the factory men whose suggestions for improving our product and processes had been accepted and rewarded. There were about four hundred factory men present, and I enclose the dinner menu showing the results for the year and the factory officials on the Board that reviewed the work.

"You will note we received 1,615 suggestions for improvement in our product and the surprising thing about these suggestions is that we adopted 389 of them, over 25 percent, which you will appreciate is very high calibre of practical thinking. The minimum award paid by the Board is $5 and there is no limit on the maximum.

"During the reading of this report and the talks of the evening my thoughts were directed to the accomplishments of the factory organization and the unusually fine products they have been producing and I was very pleased and could realize why we were making such fine improvements in our products and methods…

"Our factories are acknowledged to be the best equipped plants for scientific and economical manufacture of tires. With an organization all stockholders—concentrating their entire energy to the production of better tires—with the firm policy of the company over a period of years to give the greatest value for the least amount of money I cannot help but feel that, if the sales organization could get that thought across to the consumers of tires in a convincing way, my promise to the factory organization would be more than fulfilled."

This was written when business was good:

"In reading over the branch managers' letters for January, it is very encouraging to note the optimism and enthusiasm as to what you felt the future held forth for you. In contrast to that, however, it is rather discouraging to look at your distribution and sales. I would not want to dampen or slow down your enthusiasm or optimism in any way, as success depends so much on both of these, yet I want you to realize that optimism and enthusiasm are very dangerous and disappointing unless you have a good foundation based upon knowledge and a plan on which you can and are determined to realize upon them."

Selling is not a matter of systems but of men, and we have found that a salesman cannot get the right knowledge to sell tires without going through a tire course at Akron. To this course I have given a great deal of attention, as also I have to the other course for college men which is elsewhere described—for both are in the line of men building. Tire salesmen have to be made because they must know tires. A first-class salesman who can make a record number of sales has possibilities of being a liability to us unless he knows the construction of tires and the proper uses of the different types so that he may instruct the dealers, who, in turn may impart this knowledge to the consumer. That is why we began our school for salesmen, which lasts from two to three months and is held in the factory at Akron.

The salesmen-pupils are usually picked by the branch managers and sent in, but sometimes we pick them ourselves from the factory or office organization. We are very careful in selecting our men—they must be willing to work.

The class goes into every detail of tire making and tire service. At first, we had an instructor lecture to the men—we try to avoid having more than twenty-five in a class—but we found not all the men got what they were expected to get, and now the classes are informal. The instructor brings up a subject and tries to have the men ask questions as they go along. They master the idea of all the factory operations, but we do not require them to learn to build tires. We do require them to repair all classes of tires, to put on and take off tires, and learn all that a first-class service and repair man ought to know. When these men leave the class, they know our tires and how to talk them. It is more important for a salesman to be able to sell exactly the right tire and to explain why he is selling it than to be able to make a tire.

The cost of this training is fairly heavy, but it pays. It is hard for an untrained salesman to make much of a showing for the first several months, and he is likely to become discouraged and leave, and we lose what knowledge he has secured. A trained man who goes into the field with confidence and a knowledge of his goods can do well almost from the start. This has shown in a decreased turnover of 17 percent since the school graduates began to reach the field. Our records prove that a graduate will, in his first months of actual selling, average 74 percent better than an untrained man. With a 17 percent decrease in salesman turnover, we have thus gained eighty-five men in the over one-year group. This means an average of more than two hundred and thirty-five thousand dollars in additional monthly sales on our present business, or the equivalent of twenty-four average salesmen.

And this, I take it, is conclusive as to the value of putting some money into education.

160 " But then, successful business is never conducted on rules; it is conducted on principles put into effect by human energy."

Chapter XIII
Camping with Edison, Ford, and Burroughs

Among the larger events of my life I must record the camping trips which I was privileged to take with Thomas A. Edison, Henry Ford, and John Burroughs. We had seven of these trips in nine years—although two were not strictly camping trips, but rather little journeys from an established headquarters. On four of them we had John Burroughs. On another came President Harding for a couple of days. On our last trip, which was in 1924, we visited President Coolidge at his old home in New Hampshire. We may not have any more camping trips, for, while Mr. Edison and Mr. Ford are as much disposed as ever for the outdoors and would like to go as we used to go, the publicity which the trips began to gather around them eliminated their object and charm. We were never free. Instead of a simple, gipsy-like fortnight on the road, we found ourselves in the midst of motion-picture operators, reporters, and curiosity seekers. We became a kind of travelling circus and, although all of us were accustomed to a degree of publicity, it became tiresome to be utterly without privacy.

And so this may be a final—and the only—record of our wanderings, and I want to set down, partly in my own words and partly in the words of others, something about Thomas A. Edison and Henry Ford, for they certainly own the most outstanding sets of brains in the world today. I doubt if any two men ever contributed more to the public welfare than have they, although that may not be as generally appreciated as it ought to be.

I have always liked to be with big men—with men whose ideas extend beyond the little things near at hand and whose vision has no horizon. Both Mr. Edison and Mr. Ford, while giving attention to things near at hand, paint their big thoughts on a far-flung canvas. They have long since passed the point where they give much heed to their personal fortunes. Neither man has the slightest regard for money except for what it will do for humanity, and both have the view that the way to help humanity is to help it to help itself. They are both practical visionaries—they make their dreams come true. They are both concerned with masses of men—with those who are often, though snobbishly, called "the common people." Just as though we were not all of us plain, common people! They do not talk much about business in the usual fashion. They have nothing to say about details, not because they do not know details, but because their interests are in larger affairs.

It is hard to set down what I got from these men in a business way. But then, successful business is never conducted on rules; it is conducted on principles put into effect by human energy—by the kind of energy which does not know when it is licked. And for supreme courage and confidence no one surpasses Mr. Ford.

The idea of these trips had its birth in California in 1915 at the time of the World's Fair in San Francisco. Mr. Edison and Mr. Ford had both come out in their private cars, for the celebration of Edison Day at the fair. After an electric dinner to Mr. Edison, we looked about a bit for something to do. The electric dinner, by the way, was not a banquet on electrical food, but a banquet at which all of the food was cooked by electricity—and electrical cooking was something of a novelty at the time.

We decided to visit Luther Burbank at Santa Rosa, and ran up there in the private cars. Mr. Edison has not a keen interest in growing plants unless they fit into some invention on which he is working, although he absorbs all kinds of information for possible future use. Mr. Ford loves plants and flowers, but what took him most was the development of small garden peas all of a size, so that they might be gathered by machinery. He is always interested in substituting machine work for hand work.

A story has gone the rounds for some years that Mr. Ford and I had a contest at Burbank's as to who was the better salesman. It is said that we selected a rich Indian, and that Mr. Ford tried to sell him an automobile and failed, and that then I sold him a tire, not as a tire, but as a new and improved hoop for his children to play with. That never happened. Mr. Ford is not a salesman and never wanted to be. He does not think in terms of the selling which is persuasion.

Messrs. Edison and Ford were due at Los Angeles and were to go on from there to Edison Day at the San Diego exposition, but they thought that they were being somewhat commercialized and wanted to get away from crowds. I suggested that we leave the private cars at Riverside and proceed leisurely by automobile. That suited Mr. Edison exactly, for he likes to ride in a motor—as long as he can ride in the front seat. He has no use for any other part of a motor car! As we got off the train to take the automobiles, we found a battery of motion-picture cameras lined up to greet us. Remember, the motion picture of 1915 was not what it is today. One of the directors asked me—I found shortly that I was the manager of the party:

"You will go right by our studio. Will you stop and see these pictures as developed?"

We agreed to stop if the studio was really on our way. It proved to be, and we did stop. Then the head of the concern asked Mr. Edison to lay the corner stone of a new building which they were about to erect, and he agreed. But we were not prepared for the brass band which came out of the air to escort us five hundred feet to the site. But Mr. Edison went through with the thing—band and all. And then we stayed over at the studio a while to see a picture being made—none of us had ever seen a picture in the making.

The school children, the next day, wanted to see Mr. Edison; they lined the roads and threw flowers. And it pleased him, and he agreed to motor about to most of the schools on condition that he would not have to say anything. Mr. Edison rarely makes a speech.

Eventually, we reached San Diego, and—although Mr. Edison did not arrive until four o'clock in the afternoon for Edison

Day—the crowds were enormous. He gave a reception in the exposition grounds to the children, and as they passed, each tossed a bunch of flowers at him until, at the end, he was in a waist-high drift of flowers.

Both Mr. Ford and Mr. Edison were deeply interested in the water-power potentialities of California, and I rather think that Mr. Ford's extensive hydro-electric development dates from that trip. It was Mr. Edison's thought that, if only we had enough cheap power, we should be able to reduce manufacturing costs to a minimum and bring on widespread prosperity.

At the San Diego Exposition were many tractors, and Mr. Ford was then about to start production on his tractor. He did not start as he had scheduled because, when we entered the war, he sent all the tractors he could produce to England to plough up the country and produce food. They both thought that the "caterpillar" tractor was bad in that there was too much wear on the cogs. But both were certain that the work of the farm would eventually be done by machinery, although Mr. Edison favoured the electric motor and Mr. Ford the gas engine. One day, when we passed a train of ploughs drawn by sixteen horses, Mr. Ford remarked:

"That is going to be done by machinery."

Today it is done by machinery.

Mr. Ford was at the time, it may be remembered, very active in prison work—that is, he was taking men into his shops from the prisons and had made something in the nature of a standing offer to employ any convict just out of prison. We visited the San Quentin prison and had lunch. The convicts had all heard of the plan. They called on Mr. Ford for a speech—and he does not make speeches. Mr. Ford is reported to have said:

"Glad to see you all here."

But—to spoil a good story—he said nothing of the sort. He merely rose and bowed.

We had been entertained so much that I thought it was up to someone to give a return dinner, and that the someone was I. Mr. Edison does not like to put on evening dress. He has a prejudice against what he calls "dudes." Mr. Ford and Mr. Burbank had much the same feeling. So a formal dinner was out of the question. With the help of the manager of the Fairmount Hotel, I got up a Hawaiian dinner, bringing up a fine Hawaiian band and a group of dancers. The dancers did not go on—I got a bit worried about them!

But we had a good time—so good a time that, when the party broke up, Mr. Ford hired the whole band and their families and took them off to Detroit to play and to work.

Mr. Edison went home by way of the Grand Canon, while I stayed in California to look after business. All of us had such a good time that Mr. Edison proposed that the three of us go camping the next year. Mr. Edison was to decide where we should go. He has always chosen the route. First, he writes to us, giving the route. Then he writes again, giving another route, and when we actually start, he commonly selects a third route. We never know where we are going, and I suspect that he does not, either. He rides in the front seat of the front car and directs the caravan by compass. He dislikes paved roads, and never does he select a main highway if he can find a by-way. And never does he take us into a large town if he can find another way around. When he thinks we have gone far enough, he decides to camp, and then we camp.

But he is not a hard leader, for he does not insist upon getting out early in the morning. The chief trouble is in getting him to bed. He likes to sit up until at least midnight, talking by the camp fire. And he is an exceedingly interesting talker, for not only is he a good story-teller but he has a marvellous range of information. He reads a great deal and he remembers what he reads, so that he can talk deeply on any subject· As everyone knows, he is an indomitable worker, but when he is on vacation he does not try to work. He does exactly what he pleases; he goes to bed late and rises late, and whenever there is nothing else to do, he either goes to sleep or reads any newspaper he can find. He is lost without a newspaper.

When 1916 came around, we had a deal of correspondence, the upshot of which was that I should meet Mr. Edison at his place at East Orange and then motor to somewhere known only to Mr. Edison. I knew that Mr. Ford and Mr. Burroughs were to go along, but not where and when we should meet them. No one, to tell the absolute truth, wanted to go very much except Mr. Edison. He liked roughing it.

As chief of the commissary, I took along a good cook and plenty of provisions. Mr. Edison provided the equipment, to which he had given a deal of thought and of which he was very proud. His special pride was a storage battery arrangement for lighting the camp and the tents by electricity. We used that on all our trips afterward, and it worked perfectly.

It was raining hard on the morning that we were due to start from East Orange, and we delayed a while, but eventually we got off, and before nightfall it had cleared. We made our first camp by a creek, and no sooner had we settled than a farmer came along to know what we were doing there and to say that, whatever we were doing, we had better get off. I told him that Mr. Edison was one of the party, but that did not mean anything to him. He allowed that he never let any tramps or gipsies stay around on his land, even if one of them was named Edison. We settled it by giving him five dollars—which was what he was after.

The next day was wet and cold. We arrived at Woodchuck Lodge at five in the afternoon and made camp in the orchard. We found John Burroughs little inclined to go along. He said he was too old and that he was through with journeys.

Both Mr. Ford and Mr. Edison were very fond of John Burroughs, probably because he came from a different world. He was as a child, knowing and caring nothing about business or money. His whole interest was in the trees and the birds and the half-wild life about him. I think Mr. Ford found a common bond with him in a love for birds; not many men know more about birds than does Mr. Ford. Mr. Edison, I think, liked Burroughs not only for himself, but with his passion for knowledge of all kinds, he wanted a man along who could tell us about the trees and the birds and the flowers.

There was no convincing Burroughs that he should come along—that is, before dinner. But the cook did himself extremely well that night, and when we were through, Mr. Burroughs suddenly announced that he would join us in the morning. When we reached Albany, I telephoned Mr. Ford, and he said that he would meet us two or three days later at a point we gave him. There we found a wire from him saying he could not come.

We journeyed up through the Adirondacks and almost into Canada. Then we turned back through Vermont, coming home through Rutland, Pittsfield, Amenia, and Poughkeepsie, dropping Mr. Burroughs on the way and reaching East Orange at three o'clock in the afternoon of September 9th, having covered 1,115 miles.

We usually camped out, and some of these country people are thrifty! One noon, in northern New York, we stopped inside the fence of what seemed to be an abandoned farmhouse. No one was around, and the house was half ruined. Hardly had we started lunch when a couple of ladies drove up. They had an air of possession.

"Excuse me," I asked, "do you object to our having lunch here?"

"Yes," answered one flatly.

"Do you own the property?" I replied, somewhat nettled.

"No, but it belongs to our grandmother."

"Well, then, tell us how much damage we are doing and I'll pay you."

They went off without answering, but hardly had they gone when a big load of hay came driving in—and we had set our table in the road.

"Hey," yelled Mr. Edison, "can't you wait a bit?"

"I dunno," answered the driver, "this load is pretty heavy."

"Will you wait half an hour for two dollars?"

"Yes," he answered. Then he took the money and, with a grin, drove around us.

Mr. Edison not only planned the trip, but he made rules for it. One of these rules was that no one should shave. On a cold night on the Ausable, we decided that Mr. Burroughs had better not sleep out, and I drove him over to a hotel in Ausable Forks—two miles away—leaving Mr. Edison and my son Harvey in camp. When I saw the hotel bedroom and bath I could stand the strain no longer and I struck. Not only did I have a shave and a bath, but also I spent the night comfortably in a bed.

168

I did not know what was going to happen when I reached camp in the morning with Mr. Burroughs and found Mr. Edison and Harvey alone at breakfast. Mr. Edison saw at once that I had shaved. He did not so much mind having me out all night, but he did not like that shave—the breaking of the rules.

"You're a tenderfoot," he laughed. "Soon you'll be dressing up like a dude."

But Mr. Edison is seldom in a bad humour. He forgets every care and worry.

Later in the year, Mr. Burroughs wrote Mr. Edison and me a letter which sums up the trip better than I can:

"My DEAR EDISON AND FIRESTONE:

"That was a fine trip you gave us. John Muir would have called it a glorious trip. You arranged the weather just right and you begot in all of us the true holiday spirit. We were out on a lark and our spirits soared and sang like larks most of the time. My health had been so precarious during the summer that I feared I could not stand more than two or three days of the journey, but, as it turned out, the farther I went the farther I wanted to go. I drank in health and strength every hour. The doctors think that, as we grow old, there is great remedial power in mechanical vibrations. I think the vibrations of a motor car over the good state roads on a trip to the Adirondacks with such a company in it as we had beats all other appliances. But the vibrations or convulsions set up in the diaphragm by the stories around the camp fire at night beat even that, or at least supplement it in a most effective way. I do not know which I owe the most to—the camp fires or the car. I am only sure that I took a most delightful shaking up—such as I had not had for forty years. It is true that it does not take much to make one laugh on such occasion; he is in the jocose spirit—and a little humour goes a good way. We see life at an unaccustomed angle, and the droll side of it strikes us with unaccustomed force.

"'Well, I say à la Muir we had a glorious trip. We cut the heart out of the Adirondacks, and we took a big slice off the Green Mountains. I had never before seen the Adirondacks under such favourable conditions. Seen as we saw them, lined up in a great procession, they are very impressive. They take the conceit out of my native Catskills. Their vast geologic age awes one, holding their heads so high after a hundred or more million of years, and their magnitude and primordial look-all stir the imagination. In them we beheld the source of much of the land out of which you and I came. They are the mother of vast areas of stratified rock in the lower part of the state. Here I saw the source of the vast sand and gravel and clay banks of the lower Hudson. When Edison gets his foundry perfected for extracting potash on a commercial scale out of the granite rocks, what an inexhaustible supply the Adirondacks will afford him. In one of your pictures, where Edison and I are half hidden in the grass, he has his hands full of disintegrated granite and is pointing out to me and naming the different mineral elements it contains and telling me of their various uses. The feldspar is the source of the potash which he hopes to obtain on a scale that will make us independent of the Germans for this mineral.

"It was a great pleasure to see Edison relax and turn vagabond so easily, sleeping in his clothes, curling up at lunch time on a blanket under a tree and dropping off to sleep like a baby, getting up to replenish the camp fire at daylight or before, making his toilet at the creek or wayside pool, and more than that, to see him practise what he preaches about our excessive eating, and at each meal taking only a little toast and a cup of hot milk. The luxuries of our 'Waldorf-Astoria' on wheels that followed us everywhere had little attraction for Mr. Edison. One cold night, you remember, he hit on a new way of folding his blankets; he made them interlock so and so, then got into them, made one revolution, and the thing was done. Do you remember with what boyish delight he would throw up his arms when we suddenly came upon some particularly striking view? I have to laugh when I think of the incident of the big car two girls were driving down a wet, slippery street in Saranac and which, when the driver put on the brakes, suddenly changed ends and stopped, leaving the amazed girls looking up the street instead of down. 'Organized matter,' remarked Mr. Edison, 'sometimes behaves in a very strange manner.'

"Such a trip is a very sane and hygienic way of spending a brief vacation, especially if you keep clear of houses and hotels as we did, and have so well-organized an expedition as we had. The thought of it and the joy of it and the good of it stay with one for many a day.

"Gratefully yours,

"JOHN BURROUGHS."

We had all planned for a trip in 1917, but the coming of the war found us with our hands too full to take any time off for gadding about, and it was not until 1918 that we had our next trip—and it was the best that we had ever had.

172   " Mr. Firestone belongs to an entirely
       different type—the clean, clear-headed,
       conscientious business type, always on
       his job, always ready for whatever comes,
       always at the service of those around him. "

Chapter XIV

Camping Through the Smoky Mountains and the Shenandoah Valley

Our 1918 trip was, as I have said, the best of all. Mr. Ford came down to our old homestead at Columbiana and, on August 18th, Mr. Ford, Harvey, Jr., and I met Mr. Edison, Mr. Burroughs, and his friend Professor De Loach at Pittsburgh. The war was on. Excepting Mr. Burroughs, we were all head over heels in war work, but we had decided that a couple of weeks off would freshen us all a bit and make us better able to go on with our work.

Our route—or Mr. Edison's route, for the rest of us did not know where we were going—turned out to be down through the Smoky Mountains into West Virginia, Tennessee, and as far south as Asheville, North Carolina, and back through the Shenandoah Valley to Hagerstown, Maryland, where we disbanded.

John Burroughs wrote out for us, when he returned home, an account of his impressions. It gives a far better narrative than I can give, and he writes from a very different viewpoint. This is his story in part:[1]

"I was fairly enlisted and bound to see the Old Smokies. They were a strong lure to Mr. Edison, who has many years yet to wait before he can graduate as an octogenarian. More than that, he is always in need of an outing, and of a shaking up as an antidote to his concentrated life. As for Mr. Ford, Mr. Firestone, and Professor De Loach, the keen edge of youth has not yet been blunted in them, only dulled a little here and there, perhaps, so that in trying to keep step with these boys I was at a great disadvantage.

---

[1]

Mr. Burroughs included this account in a volume entitled, *Under the Maples*, under the title "A Strenuous Holiday," and these extracts are used by the permission of the publishers, Houghton Mifflin Company.

"The preliminary drive with Edison and De Loach from Orange, New Jersey, to Pittsburgh, nearly four hundred miles in two days, was, for me, too big a dose at the outset. In our furious speed, the car fairly kicked up its heels at times, and we were unseated all too often. It was not easy to unseat Mr. Edison beside the chauffeur—there is a good deal of him to unseat, and he is cushiony and adjustable, and always carries his own shock absorbers with him. My own equipment of this sort disappeared long ago, and I am very sensitive on the subject of hard driving....

"Pittsburgh is a city that sits with its feet in or very near the lake of brimstone and fire, and its head in the sweet country air of the hilltops. I think I got nearer the infernal regions there than I ever did in any other city in this country. One is fairly suffocated, at times, driving along the public highways on a bright, breezy August day. It might well be the devil's laboratory. Out of such blackening and blasting fumes comes our civilization. That weapons of war and destructiveness should come out of such pits and abysses of hell fire seemed fit and natural, but much more comes out of them—much that suggests the pond lily rising out of the black slime and muck of the lake bottoms.

"We live in an age of iron and have all we can do to keep the iron from entering our souls. Our vast industries have their root in the geologic history of the globe as in no other past age. We delve for our power, and it is all barbarous and unhandsome. When the coal and oil are all gone and we come to the surface and above the surface for the white coal, for the smokeless oil, for the winds and the sunshine, how much more attractive life will be! Our very minds ought to be cleaner. We may never hitch our wagons to the stars, but we can hitch them to the mountain streams and make the summer breezes lift our burdens. Then the silver age will displace the iron age....

"At Pittsburgh our party was finally made up by the accession of Mr. Ford, Mr. Firestone, and his son, Harvey, and Commissioner Hurley of the Shipping Board. Mr. Hurley was to be with us only a few days to taste for himself the sweet and the bitter of roughing it—the promise which had lured his friends,

Edison and Ford, into such an expedition. I hope he got a good mouthful of the sweet, at least that first night in our camp at Greensborough, thirty or more miles southeast of Pittsburgh. The camp was in an ideal place—a large open oak grove on a gentle eminence well carpeted with grass, with wood and water in abundance. But the night was chilly and I got more of the bitter than of the sweet. But I had been a prophet of evil from the start, and it was fit that I should justify myself the first night. Folding camp cots are very poor conservers of one's bodily warmth, and until you get the hang of them and equip yourself with plenty of blankets, sleep enters your tent very reluctantly. She tarried with me but briefly, and at three or four in the morning I got up, replenished the fire, and in a camp chair beside it indulged in the 'long, long thoughts' which belong to age much more than to youth. Youth was soundly and audibly sleeping in the tents with no thoughts at all. I trust Mr. Hurley was doing his share of it with no visions of sinking ships troubling his dreams.

"Not much of the talk that night around the camp fire can be repeated, but it gave us an inside view of many things we were curious about. The ship question was the acute question of the hour, and we had with us the man who could give us first-hand information, which he did, to our great comfort.

"How could we help freeing our minds about the Huns!

"'We must win,' Mr. Ford said, 'and to do it we shall have to use up a lot of our resources. It is all waste, but it seems necessary, and we are ready to pay the price.' "We christened this our first camp, Camp Hurley, in honour of our guest.

"The next day one of the big cars—a Packard—had an accident—the fan broke and the iron punctured the radiator. It looked for the moment as if we should be delayed till a new radiator could be forwarded from Pittsburgh. We made our way slowly to Connellsville, where there is a good garage, but the best workmen there shook their heads; they said a new radiator was the only remedy. All four arms of the fan were broken off, and there was no way to mend them. This verdict put Mr. Ford on his mettle.

"'Give me a chance,' he said. Pulling off his coat and rolling up his sleeves, he fell to work. In two hours we were ready to go ahead. By the aid of drills and copper wire, the master mechanic had stitched the several arms on their stubs, soldered up the hole in the radiator, and the disabled car was again in running order.

"At Connellsville, Mr. Hurley felt compelled to leave us to attend a cabinet meeting in Washington on Tuesday. A keen and competent government official, we all agreed; whether Republican or Democrat, who cared? In such times as these party lines do not count. We are only loyal and patriotic American citizens.

"On Tuesday night, August twenty-first, we made our camp on the banks of a large, clear creek in West Virginia, called Horse Shoe Run. A smooth field across the road from the creek seemed attractive, and I got the reluctant consent of the widow that owned it to pitch our camp there, though her patch of roasting ears nearby made her hesitate; she had probably experience with gipsy parties, and the two magic names which I gave her of men in our party did not impress her. But Edison was not attracted by the open field, the rough grassy margin of the creek suited him better, and its proximity to the murmuring, eddying, rocky current appealed to us all, albeit our mess tent was pitched astride a gully and our individual tents elbowed each other in the narrow spaces between the boulders.

"An interesting object near our camp was an old, unused grist mill, with a huge decaying overshot oaken water wheel.

"At our lunch that day, by the side of a spring, a twelve-year-old girl appeared in the road above us with a pail of apples for sale. We invited her into our camp, an invitation she timidly accepted. We took all of her apples. I can see her yet, with her shining eyes, as she crumpled the new one-dollar bill which Mr. Ford placed in her hand. She did not look at it, the feel of it told the story to her. We quizzed her about many things and got straight, clear-cut answers—a very firm, levelheaded little maiden. Her home was on the hill above us. We told her the names of some of the members of the party, and after she had returned home, we saw an aged man come out to the gate and look down upon us. An added human interest was given to the trip whenever we came in contact with any of the local population. Birds and flowers and trees and spring and mills were something, but human flowers and rills of human life were better. I do not forget the other maiden, twelve or thirteen years old, to whom we gave a lift of a few miles on her way. She had been on a train five times, and once had been forty miles from home. Her mother was dead and her father lived in Pennsylvania. She was living with her grandfather. When asked how far it was to Elkins, she said:

"'Ever and ever so many miles.'

"August twenty-third, we made camp at Bolar Springs—a famous spring, and a beautiful spot. We pitched our tents among the sugar maples, and some of the party availed themselves of the public bathhouse that spanned the overflow of the great spring. At breakfast, I heard someone ask Mr. Edison if he would have prunes.

177

"'No,' he said. 'I was once a telegraph operator and lived in a boarding house.'

"I think it was here that Mr. Edison gave several children standing about a nickel each. When asked if they knew his name, a little girl answered, 'Yes, Mr. Graphophone.'

"August twenty-fourth, we made camp on Wolf Creek, not far from the Narrows. Mr. Firestone said to Mr. Edison:

"'This is the first place we have struck where they don't know any of us.'

"'Good!' said Mr. Edison. 'We shall have a good time here.' Mr. Edison shrank from publicity at all times.

"We were on the narrow grassy margin of a broad, limpid creek in which the fish were jumping, a beautiful spot, marred only by the proximity of the dusty public highway. After our camp was made, an automobile went by and a woman's voice inside was heard to exclaim: 'What in hell is that?'

"When we have settled on a camping site, Mr. Edison settles down in his car and reads or meditates, Mr. Ford seizes an axe and swings it vigorously till there is enough wood for the camp fire.

"One privation we suffered which I think Mr. Edison and I felt more than did the others, was the scanty or delayed war news. Local papers, picked up here and there, gave us brief summaries, and here and there at the larger railroad towns we were able to get hold of Cincinnati, Philadelphia, or New York dailies, a day or two old. Persons who have hung on the breath of the great dailies for four years miss something when they are cut off from them.

"Such a trip as we were taking was, of course, a kind of lark, especially to the younger members of the party—Mr. Ford, Mr. Firestone and his son, and others. Upon Alleghany Mountain, near Barton, West Virginia, a farmer was cradling oats on a side hill below the road. Our procession stopped, and the two irrepressible youths were soon taking turns in trying their hands at cradling oats, with doubtful success. One of the pictures shows Mr. Ford and the farmer with broad smiles on their face watching Mr. Firestone with the fingers of his cradle tangled in the oats, he with a smile on his face also, but decidedly an equivocal smile—the trick was not so easy as it looked. Evidently Mr. Ford had not forgotten his cradling days on the home farm in Michigan. When it came to raking and binding I felt at home myself, as I had done it in my youth. Had it been cotton picking or planting, I presume Professor De Loach would have been moved to try his hand, as his youth was passed in Georgia.

"Camp life is a primitive affair, no matter how many conveniences you have, and things of the mind keep pretty well in the background. Occasionally, around the camp fire, we drew Edison out on chemical problems and heard formula after formula come from his tongue as if he were reading them from a book. As a practical chemist, he perhaps has few, if any, equals in this country. It was easy to draw Mr. Ford out on mechanical problems; there is always pleasure and profit in hearing a master discuss his own art. As the head of an important division of the Armour Company, and a lifelong student of physics and agriculture, and a student of plant pathology, De Loach was a storehouse of much valuable and interesting information. I was the only literary man in the party, and was a kind of referee in such matters. But automobile travelling shakes my wits down like a bag of corn, and it is an effort for me to get up an interest in literary subjects.

"But when Mr. Edison said he thought the two greatest works of poetry and fiction in his time were 'Evangeline' and 'Les Misérables,' I could not agree with him. One morning, Mr. Edison asked me if Shakespeare could be reproduced, without loss, in common everyday speech; if it could not, he evidently thought it so much against him. I told him it was hard to put any piece of pure literature into other language without loss.

179

"By a mere chance I had with me Channing's book on Thoreau. As we had little other reading matter, Edison delved into it a good deal. He asked me if Thoreau did not overdo the matter, and whether or not Channing was a good writer. I replied that I considered Channing a clumsy, ineffectual writer, and that his book on Thoreau was of little value; that Thoreau himself was an extreme, uncompromising idealist, and stroked the world the wrong way of the fur, but that the value of his contribution to American literature ranked next to that of Emerson's.

"At the time of our trip, the people of Michigan were talking about sending Mr. Ford to the Senate. Mr. Ford said he has no ambition that way, but that if Edison would go from New Jersey they might together do something. One of the things they would do would be to move for the repeal of the patent laws. It was surprising to learn that neither of them had been benefited by the patent laws. The inventor himself, they said, rarely gets any benefit from them; it is the capitalists that make the money. But Edison did not crave political honours; he said he was like Faraday who, when they wanted to make him a knight, said:

"'I was born plain Faraday, and I want to die plain Faraday.'

"He said he didn't want to go to the Senate and that there was 'nothing in being President.'

"'When Ford goes to the Senate,' he declared, 'he will be mum; he won't say a damn word.'

"Edison said he was too deaf. Ford replied:

"'It isn't what you hear that makes you useful, it's what you do or say—what you tell the people.'

"Our two chief characters presented many contrasts: Mr. Ford is more adaptive, more indifferent to places, than is Mr. Edison. His interest in the stream is in its potential water power. He races up and down its banks to see its fall, and where power could be developed. He is never tired of talking of how much power is going to waste everywhere, and says that if the streams were all harnessed, as they could easily be, farm labour everywhere, indoors and out, could be greatly lessened. He dilates upon the benefit that would accrue to every country neighbourhood if the water power that is going to waste in its valley streams were set to work in some useful industry, furnishing employment to the farmers and others in the winter season when their farms need comparatively little of their attention.

"Mr. Ford always thinks in terms of the greatest good to the greatest number. He aims to place all his inventions within the reach of the great mass of the people. When he first went into the automobile business he associated himself with others in building a large, expensive car, but very soon saw that the need was for a car sufficiently low in price to place it within the reach of the mass of the population. In building his tractor engine, he has had the same end in view, so that now there is a machine on the market the price of which places it within reach of nearly as many farmers as is the car. He does not forget the housewife either, and has plans for bringing power into every household that would greatly lighten the burden of the womenfolk. The old-fashioned grist mills along the road, with their huge overshot wheels, were of never-failing interest to him.

"The behaviour of Mr. Edison on such a trip is in marked contrast to that of Mr. Ford. Partly owing to his much greater age, but mainly, no doubt, to his more meditative and introspective cast of mind, he is far less active. When we paused for midday lunch, or to make camp at the end of the day, Mr. Edison would sit in his car reading, or curl up, boy fashion, under a tree and take a nap, while Mr. Ford would inspect the stream or busy himself in getting wood for the fire. Mr. Ford is a runner and a high kicker, and frequently challenges some member of the party to race with him. He is also a persistent walker, and from every camp, both morning and evening, he sallied forth for a brisk half-hour walk. His cheerfulness and adaptability on all occasions, and his optimism in regard to all the great questions, are remarkable. His goodwill and tolerance are as broad as the world. Notwithstanding his practical turn of mind, and his mastery of the mechanic arts and of business methods, he is through and through an idealist. This combination of powers and qualities makes him a very interesting and, I may say, lovable personality. He is as tender as a woman, and much more tolerant. He looks like a poet, and conducts his life like a philosopher. No poet ever expressed himself through his work more completely than Mr. Ford has expressed himself through his car and his tractor engine they typify him—not imposing, nor complex, less expressive of power and mass than of simplicity and adaptability and universal service.

"Those who meet Mr. Ford are almost invariably drawn to him. He is a national figure, and the crowds that flock around the car in which he is riding, as we pause in the towns through which we pass, are not paying their homage merely to a successful car-builder, or business man, but to a beneficent human force, a great practical idealist, whose goodwill and spirit of universal helpfulness they have all felt. He has not only brought pleasure and profit into their lives, but has illustrated and written large upon the pages of current history a new ideal of the business man—that of a man whose devotion to the public good has been a ruling passion, and whose wealth has inevitably flowed from the depth of his humanitarianism. He has taken the people into partnership with him and has eagerly shared with them the benefits that are the fruit of his great enterprise—a liberator, an emancipator, through channels that are so often used to enslave or destroy.

"In one respect, essentially the same thing may be said of Mr. Edison—he has become wealthy in spite of himself, through his great service to the whole civilized world. His first and leading thought has been, What can I do to make life easier and more enjoyable to my fellow men? He is a great chemist, a trenchant and original thinker on all the great questions of life—a practical scientist, plus a meditative philosopher of profound insight. We all delighted in his wise and witty sayings.

"He is a good camper-out and turns vagabond very easily. He can go with his hair uncombed and his clothes unbrushed as long as the best of us. He eats so little that I do not think he was tempted by the chicken roosts or turkey flocks along the way, nor by the corn fields and apple orchards, as some of us were. But there can be no doubt about his love for the open air and for wild nature. He can rough it week in and week out and be happy.

"Mr. Firestone belongs to an entirely different type—the clean, clear-headed, conscientious business type, always on his job, always ready for whatever comes, always at the service of those around him, a man devoted to his family and his friends, sound in his ideas, and generous of the wealth that has come to him as a manufacturer who has faithfully and honestly served his countrymen.

"When a man of letters like myself goes a junketing with two such well-known men as Edison and Ford, he shines mainly by reflected light—he is in famous company. The public is eager to press the hand and hear the voice of these two men, but a writer of books excites interest only now and then. School-teachers, editors, doctors, clergymen, lawyers, nature lovers, frequently gravitate to my side of the car, while the main crowd of working and business men goes to the other side. I felt pretty sure of the schools, but once in a town in North Carolina I miscalculated. A big band of college girls swarmed up to our car, and the president of the college was with them. He turned to his pupils and said:

"'Ladies of the college, this is Henry Ford.'

"Mr. Ford stood up and made his best bow. I sat there smiling and expectant, but the 'ladies of the college' will never know by what a close shave I missed fame at that moment. I was in total eclipse. I had my little speech ready on my tongue. I was going to say: "'Ladies of the college, I write books, and Mr. Ford makes cars; I hope you will read my books and ride in nothing but Ford cars.'

183

"Brief enough, surely, and to the point, but it perished on my tongue, and but for this record, the world and the 'ladies of the college' would never know how quickly my mental barometer fell from high to low on that occasion."

The chauffeur of one of our cars also took a hand at writing some of the incidents of this trip—some that the mind of Mr. Burroughs did not note. Here are a few extracts—out of their chronological order, which makes not the least difference:

"One said we were going right; others voted nay. All of which did not seem to interest Mr. Edison at all, for right in the middle of the pro-and-conning, he said, quite suddenly:

"'I've just got to get a bottle of pop somewhere. Wonder where's the best place to go? Got any idea, Harvey?'

"Harvey, Jr., drove over the hill somewhere, and almost as quickly and mysteriously as the good genii in the fairy tale, fetched the pop for which Mr. Edison had wished—and fetched back with him, also, the news that we were then within the confines of that noble but invisible metropolis, Kaiser's Ridge. We were there but we didn't know it…"

And this is his account of the broken fan which Mr. Burroughs referred to:

"Just as we were slipping along nice and cozily into Connells-ville, my fan iron broke and punctured the radiator, and Mr. Ford, Mr. Hurley, and Mr. Firestone had to pile out while I crawled around under the hood and tried to coax her to get to going again. Here, I am confiding to you, is where my corre-spondence-school training certainly left me in the lurch. That broken fan iron and punctured radiator absolutely refused to let me put them on a working basis again, and finally I had to admit that the problem was too much for me.

"Then Henry Ford stepped up, business-like, took off his coat, rolled up his sleeves and went to it like a real mechanic who knows his job and is anxious to get to tinkering around in the machinery. Mr. Ford was anxious to get a crack at that engine, I think—anyway he took the darned thing apart, adjusted things here, and readjusted things there, and, in no time at all, he had the car running slick as a whistle and we were on our way again. All of which proves that this man Ford certainly is on intimate terms with every little bolt and nut that goes to make up an automobile—and which proves, also, that a man must know his business from the ground up before he can have twenty-five thousand people working for him—before he can convince us all that there's worse things to do than turn out millions of flivvers.

"On the way out of Elkins a spring shackle bolt, whatever that is, sheared off (that's what Mr. Firestone said it did) and it looked to me as though we were going to be laid up there on the road for at least another hour, but Mr. Ford, never to be daunted by anything mechanically cantankerous, turned his eye on a big field which lay alongside the road, spied a thresher, and while I was still mourning the loss of that shackle bolt, hiked over into the field, borrowed just exactly the bolt he wanted from the obliging threshers, and returned in a jiffy. It took two hours and a lot of work to put that spring back in good springing order again, but Mr. Ford stayed on the job until he had us going thirty-five miles an hour once more—and didn't demand a cent of overtime.

"A substantial-looking citizen, whose car 'acted up' near our camp, got the highest-paid mechanic in the world to put his bus on its feet again. When Mr. Ford had fixed the car, the man turned to him and said:

"'How much do I owe you, stranger?'

"To which Mr. Ford replied:

"'Not a cent, friend; I really don't need the money.'

"Whereupon the man looked at Mr. Ford and at the little car which Mr. Ford was driving. Then he said:

"'My good man, I insist on paying you for this work. Whether you say you need the money or not, I don't agree with you. No man would be riding in one of those little cars if he had all the money he needed!'"

185

186 "On one point I am certain—the employees ought to have some stock interest, and we have made that compulsory—a condition of employment."

Chapter XV
More Camping, some Business Philosophy, and Two Presidents

Two points which Mr. Edison and Mr. Ford dwelt on, time and again, during our talks about the camp fire, were:

1. Own your business.

2. Keep plenty of cash in bank—make the banks work for you.

Mr. Edison is a great inventive genius with a wide business experience; he has had a marvellous laboratory experience, but he is impatient of detail that is not connected with his experiments and really his largest interest is in development.

As is well known, Mr. Ford paid seventy-odd millions of dollars to buy out his minority stockholders, while Mr. Edison, who has been interested in many companies, has now full ownership and control of all his companies.

Both men want to serve the public to the largest degree, and their vision is so long and their courage so high that it would be quite impossible for any group of stockholders to keep pace with them, and especially since neither of them will take the time or the trouble to explain exactly what he is about.

Mr. Ford is both a mechanical genius and a business genius. He goes through conventions—through established practices—with a superb surety. He has the genius of reducing a problem to its elements in so simple a fashion that it does not appear to be a problem at all.

I can easily see that convincing stockholders of the rightness of this or that course, especially since it might involve the payment of a small dividend, instead of a large one, would demand the kind of argument that neither Mr. Ford nor Mr. Edison will make. I doubt if Mr. Ford could have carried out more than a fraction of his plans had his business not been personal with him and his family. For it was the building of the River Rouge plant that brought on the suits which resulted in his buying out all the stockholders. And the River Rouge plant has proved to be the longest single step in the direction of economy that he has ever taken! I agree thoroughly with Mr. Ford that one man must run a business. A business with more than one head is as monstrous as a man with more than one head. This or that business may seem to succeed for a time in the hands of a board of directors or a committee of managers, but it will always be found that either the business is really running on the momentum of the founder or, as in the 1919 boom, it is running because no one has the strength to stop it, or some one man dominates the directors or committee and is the real manager—whatever his title.

Every American business of consequence has been built up by one man staying on the job. The corporate form of organization is only a method of defining the interests of investors. It is not a form of management. And when the stockholders vigorously help in the management, the business cannot prosper.

Of late, there has been a deal of discussion about the rights of minority stockholders, but all that I have ever known minority stockholders to be really active about was the distribution of higher dividends than the business could afford—if it were to expand on other than borrowed money. An expansion on borrowed money is very dangerous. We have never made a move of real importance that has not been opposed by some stockholders. When we went into the making of pneumatic tires, we had protests, and to avoid difficulties I arranged to buy out the protesting interests. And the largest development we have considered—the true import of which is developed into a subsequent chapter—the growing of our own rubber either in Liberia, or in the Philippines, or in both—has caused protests from stockholders.

The moment that a company starts paying dividends without regard to future needs, it is as good as finished. If the number of stockholders be large, the dividends have to be high—the stock market actually judges the condition of a company by the dividends it pays. High dividends may be a sign of strength, but more often they are a sign of heedless management.

The position of Mr. Ford with respect to stockholders is certainly sound. It might be argued that with a man of less genius, the plan would not work at all. That is true, but neither would any other plan. A dull man cannot make a success of business just because he has stockholders and directors. There is nothing impersonal about a corporation—it is the most personal thing on earth. No impersonal, legal formula for successful corporate management exists.

The trouble is that the founder of a quickly growing business cannot always raise enough money out of the business itself for needed expansion. And as between issuing bonds and issuing stock, there can be no choice at all, for a funded debt is a constant menace. One who founds a business simply has to choose between expanding on the profits or expanding on the profits plus the proceeds of new issues of stock. Undoubtedly, the first course is the better, if it can be followed. The next best course is to have as few stockholders as possible and have them investors, not speculators.

189

On one point I am certain—the employees ought to have some stock interest, and we have made that compulsory—a condition of employment. And also I believe that the officers should have their savings in the company they work for. Whenever stock is offered for sale, I try to get the officers of the company in on the purchase. The best results are obtained when a majority of the stockholders are directly involved in the management of the company.

Mr. Ford, ever since his business became successful, has always carried a large cash balance. That course he has always urged upon me, and I agree with him that it is the right course, but whether or not it is wise to borrow at times cannot be decided off-hand without regard to the nature of the business. An automobile has in it only a small amount of material and a great deal of workmanship. A tire has in it a great deal of material—rubber, compounds, and cotton—and a small amount of workmanship. The rubber under present conditions has to come from far overseas—it is three months from Singapore. Once I control my sources of rubber—and that is only a few years away—I shall be able to regulate our supplies of rubber according to our business and pay little or no attention to the rubber market; the market fluctuations will be of no consequence to me. But as it is now, we have to buy according to price—although we do not speculate and this means the tying up of a deal of money.

I believe that conservative borrowing makes money for us. The ability to clean up all borrowing once a year is a test of the nature of the borrowing—although not a certain test. There are no certain tests.

Our 1919 camping trip found Mr. Ford with a new equipment for us. He insists upon having everything absolutely clean and in place. That is one of his business as well as one of his personal fundamentals. He had two cars fitted out and shining with enamel and nickel—which is the way he likes to have all machinery.

Car A, or "the kitchen cabinet car," was as fully furnished a kitchen and pantry as could be devised. Mr. Ford must have had a great deal of fun planning it. On the running board was a large gasoline stove fed from the motor tank, and inside the car was a built-in ice box and compartments for every kind of food that we needed. It was the most complete thing I have ever seen, and was so neatly fitted that the car could go forty miles an hour without a rattle.

Car B was for the camping outfit. It had compartments for each tent and bed and for everything needed to make camp. It was mounted on a truck chassis. Sato, the Japanese cook, drove the kitchen car; Fred drove the truck, and Jimmy in a Ford touring car carried anything not otherwise provided for.

My son Harvey and I met Mr. Ford at Buffalo, and at Albany on August 4th we were joined by Mr. Edison, who had driven up from Orange, and by Mr. Burroughs, who had come by train. Our first night was at Green Island, where Mr. Ford had bought a tract of land by the river to erect a hydroelectric plant. The Government had built a dam across the Hudson for some war purpose, and Mr. Ford, rather than see the power go to waste, had leased the rights.

He intended to put up a tractor plant-or, at least, he thought he might. But his principal reason for leasing was to avoid seeing so much potential power going to waste. He leased a government war dam on the Mississippi for the same purpose, and preventing waste was behind the offer which he made for Muscle Shoals—and which offer he withdrew. Where another man will build a factory and then plan to erect a power station, Mr. Ford will take the power first in the complete certainty that he can find a use for it. With him everything gets back to power. He thinks of his automobiles in terms of power.

Mr. Edison and he would dam every suitable stream in the country just to get the power. I doubt if, on our trips, we ever passed an abandoned mill without Mr. Edison and Mr. Ford getting out to measure the force of the stream, inspect the old wheel, and talk about ways and means of putting the waste power to work.

Mr. Ford has carried out this plan on the River Rouge where he has bought every abandoned mill site and already has seven of them fitted with water turbines which furnish power to small factory units.

He had not then made any plans for the factory he was to erect at Green Island, but he picked out a stone which he said would be the corner stone of the plant, and on it we all chiselled our initials.

This trip followed the same general lines as the 1916 trip. We went to Lake Placid, to Plattsburg, and after some argument as to whether or not we should go on to Montreal, we ferried down Lake Champlain and came back through Vermont, New Hampshire, Massachusetts, and Connecticut, reaching New York on August 14th.

One night, on this trip, I started to talk to Mr. Edison about rubber and its properties, and I was astounded at the knowledge of rubber that he had at hand. I had been working with rubber for many years, but he told me more than I knew and more than I think our chemists knew—although, to the best of my knowledge, Mr. Edison had never given any great attention to rubber, excepting in connection with his talking machines. But it is that way with any subject one brings up with Mr. Edison.

In 1920 we had no real trip. I went abroad early in the year, to be called back by the financial crisis which is described in a subsequent chapter. We were all very busy with finances that year, and the best that we could do was to spend a couple of days at Yama Farms and at the home of Mr. Burroughs. The only event was a tree-chopping contest at Yama Farms between Mr. Ford and Mr. Burroughs. Mr. Edison acted as timekeeper, while I refereed. We gave the victory to Mr. Burroughs. Mr. Ford, when he is out of doors, is just like a boy: he wants to have running races, climb trees, or do anything which a boy might do. He eats very little, is nearly always in first-class condition, and he likes to walk, to skate, and to dance, but he has no interest at all in any of the games such as golf. He does not object to anyone playing golf who wants to play, but he does not care for it himself.

At the Burroughs place we had a big, brigand steak that we cooked and ate outdoors in a driving snow. We cooked it in the best of all ways to cook steak, and if you do not know the way, here is the recipe.

Select a straight, green limb and sharpen the end, then cut the steak into slices and slip them over the wooden skewer with bits of bacon between the slices, and broil it over an open fire.

That was our last expedition with John Burroughs. On March 29, 1921, he died, and our next meeting was at his funeral. He was a fine man, really fine in every way, and one could not ask for a better companion—in this world but hardly of it. He was different from the rest of us in that he had nothing of the commercial instinct. The commercial instinct has been over-rated. The service instinct is more important. Neither Mr. Edison nor Mr. Ford is a trader. A mere trader does not get very far in these days. The man who looks first to service does not have to be a trader—he cannot be a trader—and only those who look first to service can now succeed. It just so happened that the way of John Burroughs led him through paths that did not produce money. He did not need money to further his service. None of us cares about money excepting as it helps us to carry out plans for larger and better service. And so, perhaps, Mr. Burroughs was not so different from us after all.

Our 1921 party was larger than ever before—we had twenty tents and a fleet of trucks, for early in the season I had asked President Harding and Mrs. Harding to come along with us—I had known the President for a long time; in fact, I first met him when he was Lieutenant Governor of Ohio. He had said that he would try to come, and so we added to our party Mrs. Edison, Mrs. Ford, Mrs. Firestone, Edsel Ford and his wife, my son Harvey and his wife, and my second son Russell. In addition, we asked Bishop and Mrs. William P. Anderson.

193

The Ford family came down to Cleveland by yacht, then motored over to Akron, and we all motored to the old homestead at Columbiana. My Aunt Nannie and the Ladies' Aid Society had a hundred chickens killed and dressed, and we loaded them in an ice box, and they made us I do not know how many cookies and cakes for our first camp with the President. And to get ahead of the story, President Harding wrote Aunt Nannie a letter telling her how much he liked those chickens and cookies and cakes. From Columbiana the Ford family and my family motored to Pittsburgh, and on July 23d we arrived at a beautiful spot picked out by Mr. Edison on Licking Creek near Hagerstown, Maryland. We were off the broad highway on a green meadow shaded by oaks and sycamores and guarded by gentle, sloping hills.

It was a Saturday, and the President was due to arrive about noon. Mr. Edison, Mr. Ford, and I set out for Funkstown to meet the President and escort him in. We did not have to wait long, for soon came a cloud of dust—President Harding was a fast driver—and in a minute or two he was out of his car and Mr. Edison and Mr. Ford, who had never met him, were being introduced. Then he got into our car, sitting on the back seat with Mr. Edison, while Mr. Ford and I sat on the folding seats. In front, with the chauffeur, was a secret service man in the seat that Mr. Edison always used. The other secret service men fallowed in the car the President had come in, while still other detectives had been sent on ahead to the camp.

President Harding had a charming manner and a rare ability to make friends. He pulled out some cigars and offered one to Mr. Edison.

"No, thank you," answered Mr. Edison. "I don't smoke, I chew." Mr. Edison does smoke a great deal, but he had the idea—I suppose—that he was not going to take a cigar just because the President offered him one. Mr. Edison does not take to everyone at once and does not pretend to. He does not set up as a hail fellow.

"I think I can accommodate you," answered the President, and with that he pulled a big plug of chewing tobacco out of his hip pocket. Mr. Edison grinned and took a big chew. Later he announced:

"Harding is all right. Any man who chews tobacco is all right."

At the camp the President took off his coat and had a turn at chopping wood, but he was no expert, and Mr. Ford finished the job. That night, around the camp fire, we had a good talk. Mr. Ford was particularly interested in the Limitation of Arms Conference on which the President was working, and we all talked it over. Mr. Ford had already made his offer for Muscle Shoals, but that we did not talk about—we kept away from everything personal. The most intense topic was a warm discussion between the President and Mr. Edison on tarpon fishing, about which both knew a great deal.

I had brought along six riding horses, and the President tried out Harbel—a magnificent Kentucky thoroughbred of which I was very proud. He wanted to ride to reduce weight, and I afterward sent on Harbel to the President and Diamond, another good horse, for Mrs. Harding, who also wanted to ride. Mrs. Harding was too ill to go with us on the trip. At the funeral of President Harding, Mrs. Harding told me how much she and the President had appreciated the horses—that the President had never allowed any one to ride Harbel other than himself—and she asked me to take them back so that they always might have the best of care.

Our life in camp with the President was very simple. The Bishop held a service in the morning, we rode horseback, and Sunday afternoon the President had to return to Washington. He had talked freely about a number of things in addition to the Arms Conference. He had spoken about the trials of being President and the vast amount of unnecessary detail imposed upon the office—which interested Mr. Ford a great deal, because Mr. Ford has worked out a way of not directly looking after anything. He also spoke of the nuisance of a President being forced to seek a second term, and thought that a single term of six years would be far better and leave the President with more time to attend to his duties. He had the feeling that it was time to stop attacking business just because it was business, and legitimate business ought to be protected and not interfered with.

195

President Harding had a real desire to be of service to the people, and so had Mrs. Harding. He cared nothing for the Presidency as such—he wanted to go down as a man who had done something for his country, and I think he had the feeling that he was not able to do more than a tiny fraction of what he wanted to do. Mr. Ford, who has a keen insight into men, was much impressed by the President's sincerity, but he doubted if he would be able to execute much of what he had projected.

Mr. Edison also grew to like him immensely. One could not help liking President Harding. He had a certain indefinable charm that drew people to him and made them like him.

After the President had left, the caravan went on to Cumberland, Maryland, and from there to Fairmount, and back to Uniontown, where it broke up on August 3d.

The start of our 1923 voyage was sad. It began at the funeral of President Harding at Marion, Ohio—Mr. and Mrs. Edison came on a few days before and visited, in Akron. From the funeral of the late President, we motored to Milan, Ohio—the birthplace of Mr. Edison, and which, for a long time, we had all been planning to see. Indeed, President Harding, when he was last with us, had proposed that some day we organize such a pilgrimage. Then we went on to Detroit. We left Detroit with our caravan on August 16th, and then, for the rest of our journey, we used sometimes the motor caravan and sometimes Mr. Ford's yacht, to see something of his great operations in northern Michigan.

On the way, we fell in with Jed Bisbee, a famous north country fiddler. At that time Mr. Ford was just becoming interested in the old dances to which he has since given so much time and thought, and at once he seized on Bisbee and we had something more than a concert, for we had the old jigs, the square dances called as they should be called, and music which none of us had heard for twenty years. Bisbee is now one of the stand-bys of the Ford dancing organization—for it has really become an organization.

We went to Iron Mountain, to the iron mines, to the logging camp at Disnaw, and to the sawmills at L'Anse. Mr. Ford owns this whole country, and he told us of his plans, which were then only being developed. But already he had cleaned up every lumber camp and put in fresh, clean buildings to replace the old shacks. The first thing which Mr. Ford does in taking over a property is to clean it up. He says that one cannot know what one has until the dirt is gotten rid of.

He had made plans for a big sawmill at Iron Mountain (it is now in operation) which would do all the woodwork for the closed bodies right at the forest and save the transport of waste lumber. He had conservation plans by which only trees over ten inches should be cut and all the brush cleared out to prevent forest fires. He had in mind also a wood distillation plant to convert the waste wood into valuable chemicals and charcoal. Of course, Mr. Edison was in his element, and he and Mr. Ford developed process after process, most of which have since been put into effect.

But the wood working and the wood saving are of themselves technical matters. The big point is that all this work was being done to save transportation of useless material, to quicken the turnover, and to earn from waste—which are three of the cardinal points in Mr. Ford's theory of manufacture.

The lesson which I learned was that a manufacturing operation should be carried through without a stop from the raw material to the finished product, and that no man can be said to control his business unless also he can control his sources. The larger the business, the greater are the possible economies.

Our last trip—1924—was scarcely a trip at all. Mrs. Ford was not able to travel by motor, and since Mr. Ford had for some time wanted us to see what he was doing at the Wayside Inn at Sudbury, Massachusetts, we adopted the Inn as a headquarters and made excursions—one to visit President Coolidge at his father's home in Plymouth, Vermont.

We met at the Inn on August 11th, and Mr. Ford showed us something of what he was doing, not only with the Inn, but with the surrounding country, much of which he has bought. His aim is to reproduce the conditions under which our forefathers lived—he believes in visual education. And so he is reconstructing the old flour mill with its overshot water wheel, has revived the village smithy, and in the course of time will have the country just as it was at the time of the Revolution— he already has oxen, wooden ploughs, and flails, and all the old tools of farming. Mr. Ford's interest in antiques is not just a form of amusement. Of course he does enjoy collecting, and at Dearborn he has an immense collection of antiques, but he has two purposes. First, he wants to see the designs of the old articles, for he has an eye to beauty; and, second, he wants people to know just what life was a hundred years or more ago. And in addition to this, it is his thought that a good idea lives forever, and he wants to examine the things of the past to see what they contained in the way of good ideas.

We had a deal of fun at the Inn. The Middlesex County farmers held their picnic there with three thousand on hand, and Mr. Ford staged for them a complete exhibition of farming from the beginnings in America to the present time. He had ox teams and tractors—every sort of farm implement from the earliest days to the present. That was only a carrying out of his theory of educating by the eye.

And then, too, we had dancing nearly every night. Mr. Ford heard that Mr. and Mrs. Benjamin Lovett of Boston knew the old dances, and they came down to teach us. Mr. Ford had liked dancing as a young man, and Mrs. Ford was also fond of it, but then he had been busy for many years with the development of his company and had no leisure at all for play. In the meantime, a new kind of dancing had come in—which he did not like. We had the old dances—the varsovienne, the schottische, the lanciers, the Virginia reel, and many others. Now the Lovetts are in Dearborn in charge of dancing.

It had been arranged that we should visit President Coolidge on the nineteenth, and on the eighteenth we started by motor and reached Ludlow, Vermont, by night—we did not camp out. The next day we went over to the old Coolidge homestead at Plymouth twelve miles away.

The President and Mrs. Coolidge came out to greet us, and with them was Colonel Coolidge, the President's father, a fine, sturdy New Englander. The house is modest in the extreme, but comfortable—a truly American home and a fitting place for a President to take his oath of office.

We talked of nothing in particular—with the motion picture cameras and the reporters we, indeed, had little time for talk, even if we had had anything to talk about. This is not to say that the President was reticent. He is supposed to be a silent man, and he is—when he has nothing to talk about. And it is a gift to keep silent when one has nothing to say!

The President gave Mr. Ford a sap bucket used by his great-great-grandfather, and on it we all wrote our names. It is now hanging in the Wayside Inn.

Then we inspected the cooperative cheese factory nearby which the President has followed closely. He explained every process of cheese making, and we all tasted cheese in its various stages—with the result that Mr. Edison, Mr. Ford, and my son Russell nursed stomach-aches that night and developed an aversion to cheese factories!

We had a few more days about New England, and then the party went its several ways. That was the last of our joint expeditions.

And out of all the trips, out of all the association with these great men, one precept stands out above all others. It has been the rule of the lives of both Mr. Edison and Mr. Ford. It is the reason why they are great. It is this:

Go it alone. Do not fail to try because someone has already tried and failed.

200 " Situations are only as impossible
as one makes them. "

Chapter XVI
Between Failure and Success

The war and its financial aftermath turned our business—and most other businesses in the country—upside down. We eventually got on our feet, and in so getting we learned so much that, although I should not like to repeat the experiences, we came out a better and sounder business than before. No business, no matter what its size, can be called safe until it has been forced to learn economy and rigidly to measure values of men and materials.

During the five years preceding the war, our factory had nearly trebled in size, and we had built a plant, which we call Plant No. 2, for the making of a single size tire. With the war we gave nearly all our output to the government for automobiles and trucks, and our new plant was turned over for the making of army balloons. I served on the Ohio Council of Defense and was a member of the Rubber Division of the War Industries Board. During 1917 and 1918 we made nearly seven million tires.

The war over, we were faced, in common with all other manufacturers, with the task of getting back to what was called "normalcy." Akron, it will be remembered, was a boom town during the war. Workmen came in by the tens of thousands to work for the various rubber companies—which were going day and night—and all of us were at our wits' end to find any sort of housing for these men. For instance, we jumped from 7,100 employees in 1916 to 10,500 employees in 1917. It was quite usual for men working nights to share a room with men working in the day. The conditions were extremely bad, but we were helpless, for the time being, to do much of anything toward making conditions better, for we were concentrated on war work. Also, we had to make new kinds of tires. Before the war, comparatively few automobiles were used for business, and the truck had not established itself as an economical form of transportation. Long hauls by trucks were unknown excepting as stunts. The war changed all that. The war was fought with trucks, and we had the problem of getting out a truck tire that would stand up under any usage.

In 1918, with the railroads clogged with government freight, I started the Ship-by-Truck movement. We were working in a great many directions and with a large force of highly paid, inefficient floaters. Those were the days when men and boys made so much more money than they had ever had before that they could see no reason for working more than a few days a week. When they had enough money they quit work and loafed, sure of another job whenever they needed it.

We did not stop work immediately after the Armistice, for we still had many government orders to fill but all of us knew that without the government as a customer we should have to make fewer tires. We saw a depression ahead and a considerable period of adjustment, for the lid had been off prices, wages, and management. We did have some depression, and there was something in the nature of an exodus of workers. We cut down our production early in 1919. Then came the boom, the biggest boom the country has ever known. During 1919, we produced more than four million tires and made a profit of more than nine million dollars. We could not keep up with demand. The railroads under government control were everywhere clogged, and everywhere dealers were paying premiums for delivery. Prices did not matter. Delivery was the thing. We bought tire fabric wherever we could get it and whenever we could get it. The machinery did not exist to turn out enough fabric for the need of the tire makers, and we had to bid against each other for fabric.

We increased our capitalization from $15,000,000 to $75,000,000 of which $40,000 000 was preferred, but it was expected that we should have to issue only $10,000,000. Every one of us felt that the boom was going to keep up, that it was the natural order of things, that we had really passed into a new kind of country and that we should have to keep pace with what was going on. On September 12, 1919, I sent out a letter which shows clearly what I thought of affairs:

"The time has come when we are faced with the necessity of deciding whether we shall stop our growth and development, or go on and keep pace with our business and expand to meet the ever-increasing demand for Firestone products.

"This was a great problem for your directors, and only after giving the matter most serious thought did they decide that it would not be fair to the stockholders of this company or to the public to limit and cut short the natural growth and development which is ahead of us. Many new fields have been opened to us, both in manufacture and in sales. As I stated at the last meeting of stockholders, the day is fast coming when competition is going to reduce the tire business to a survival of the fittest.

"I know it will be interesting to you to know why we increased our capital from $15,000,000 to $75,000,000. We contemplate selling only $10,000,000 of 7 percent preferred stock now, as that is a very large increase, and it is for the following reason:

"Less than three years ago we increased our preferred capital stock from $1,000,000 to $10,000,000. At that time, we had no thought of ever using more than $5,000,000 of the amount of preferred issue; and with that experience, and not knowing what the future might bring forth we decided to make our preferred capital stock sufficiently large so that we could issue more at any time without expense and complications and increasing it from the preferred issue of $10,000,000 to $50,000,000. It is necessary to have half as much common stock; therefore, it was necessary to increase the common stock issue to $25,000,000.

"We do not contemplate making any issue of the common stock at this time. I appreciate the desire and interest the employees have in owning stock. Our last offering was very much oversubscribed, and, if it can be arranged a little later, I hope we can make another offering. This additional capital will enable the company to do more business and will give it a greater commercial advantage and permit it to do more for its employees.

"Plant 2 was designed for a capacity of 10,000 tires a day, but we found that with additional equipment, costing between a million and a million and a half dollars, we were able to increase that capacity to 16,000 tires per day, and to convert Plant 1 from the manufacture of fabric tires to cords, and to make other similar changes, all of which required a large investment.

"One of the first things which we are planning to do is to construct a new mechanical building. This will be 325 feet long and 315 feet deep, and it will be so constructed that a part of it will be suitable for the operation of cranes over the top of big machine tools, and the balance will be occupied by other mechanical trades which do not require the heavy cranes. All of the most modern machines will be installed in this plant. Every detail of light and ventilation will be worked out. Lockers, washrooms, shower baths, and cafeteria facilities will be provided. Adjacent to this main building will be located a forge shop and a pattern storage building. These buildings, complete with heat, light, and fire protection, will cost approximately $400,000. The building now occupied by the mechanical trades will be used as a raw materials warehouse, for which it was originally designed and constructed.

"The Firestone Steel Products Company, during its first fiscal year, made sales of $5,600,000, about 45 percent of which were made to the Firestone Tire and Rubber Company. Since the signing of the Armistice, however, not only has the business of the company shown a substantial increase, but the volume of the business with outside customers has more than doubled, so that the company is now self-supporting and not dependent upon the Tire and Rubber Company.

"Indeed, its business has expanded so rapidly that its present quarters are entirely inadequate to permit it to do business on an economical and ever-increasing basis. It has, therefore, been deemed necessary to build a new plant which will be large enough to house the manufacturing equipment for making pneumatic rims. Ground has already been broken for the new plant, which will be located about one thousand feet south of Plant 2.

"The main manufacturing building of this plant will be 860 feet long by approximately 250 feet wide, and will be one story in height. The building will be of steel, brick, and concrete, and in its architecture will conform, as far as possible, to the existing building of the Tire and Rubber Company. Immediately in front of the factory will be erected a fireproof, reinforced concrete office building. This building will be two stories in height, with a basement under it in which will be located a modern cafeteria for the Steel Products Company's employees. It is expected that these buildings will be completed shortly before January 1, 1920.

"With these plans before us and the possibilities of growth open to us, it remains to be seen whether the members of the Firestone organization by their earnest efforts and loyalty to the company will make the Firestone stock as valuable to themselves as it should be."

Everything was moving and moving fast. The Ship-by-Truck movement gained tremendously. In 1916, only 215,000 trucks were registered; in 1917, the number had jumped to 326,000; in 1918, to 525,000; in 1919, to 794,372; and in 1920, the registration passed the million mark. Most of these trucks were of the ton-and-a-half variety, but others went to five tons or more. At first, we made solid tires for all trucks, but then we began the highly important development of pneumatic tires, at first only on the small trucks, but then up to trucks of three tons capacity. This required months of intensive experimenting, and we are still investigating and expect to be in research the rest of our lives—for the possibilities of the motor truck have only been touched on.

In 1919, we employed an average of 13,200 men and women and Akron had another boom—greater than the war boom. And again we had little control over the employees, because there were more jobs than men to fill them, and while we had a nucleus of old employees, we had to depend very largely on the people who turned up at the gate in the morning. We never knew in the morning how many employees we could secure for that day. In 1920, we reached a peak of 19,800 employees.

The housing of these men had become imperative. By the early part of 1919, rents had increased from 25 to 40 percent above the normal rental in other cities, and it was estimated that from 8,000 to 10,000 married men were living in the city of Akron without their families. Often as many as four men would lodge in one small room. Yet, during the first three months of 1919, only 522 permits were issued for dwellings, and 21 for apartments.

Akron was short some 5,000 houses, and, realizing the dangers of such a condition, I called together several of the more prominent business men for a housing conference. The result of this conference was the decision:

1. That a company be organized with a capitalization of $5,000,000.

2. That $2,500,000 be issued in stock at once and subscriptions obtained immediately therefor.

3. That the Goodrich Company, the Goodyear Tire & Rubber Company, and the Firestone Tire & Rubber Company each subscribe for $500,000.

4. That the other factories, merchants, business, and professional men subscribe for an additional $1,000,000.

On these lines we organized the Akron Home Owners Investment Company with these officers: H. S. Firestone, President; F. A. Seiberling, Vice President; and Dr. L. E. Sisler, Treasurer. By the first of June, 1919, more than two million dollars' worth of stock had been subscribed for.

This housing corporation was in no sense a philanthropic organization—its object was to assist people to build, at a reasonable cost, such homes as would give them a pride of ownership.

We agreed to finance individuals of good character and reputation to the extent of 90 percent of the appraised value of the lot plus the construction of the house. We had a rush of applications. We financed 469 homes, housing 491 families, or approximately 2,500 people, and our loans amounted to $2,565,167.81. In 1921, we liquidated.

Our own extensions went forward rapidly. We established at Singapore a washing and refining plant and a large warehouse. We already had a boot and shoe department, but we bought the Apsley Rubber Company at Hudson, Massachusetts, to increase our boot and shoe business. We were sitting on the top of the world.

In January of 1920, I rented a house in England, intending to spend the summer there with my family.

For it was in 1919–1920 that the presidents and other high officers of companies began to get the idea that they needed rest and recreation and plenty of it. An executive felt embarrassed if discovered within a thousand miles of his job—for of course a good executive always delegated his duties! Really, there was no managing or selling during those two years.

But somehow, after I had rented that house, I did not want to leave. Something told me that we were in a boom and that it could not last for ever. I took our 800 foremen out to the old farm and told them that, although I was always an optimist and hoped that the business would keep up, yet I had some doubts. This was in May, 1920, when business had reached its peak. I advised the foremen not to lose their heads and to be ready to slow down at any time. Then I sailed to Europe.

We had borrowed, by that time, $35,000,000 through note brokers, and we had contracted for very large amounts of rubber and fabric. The word had gone around in the tire industry that the man who could get fabric would get the business. We had never made long contracts ahead for fabric but that year we made several three-year contracts, and of course at high prices—everything was at high prices.

The sales went on fairly well through June, but in July, when the sales should have been especially good, the stock began to back up on us, and then the officers at home began to cable to me. With sales slowing down, the factories going at full speed, and materials under contract coming in, they could not make ends meet. I did not pay much attention to these cables. I knew that we were in for it, anyway, and that it would be a good thing to have a little vacation while I might.

I was on my way to Paris for a short trip when I received a cable that I could no longer put aside. It said that sales had absolutely stopped, that the officers had borrowed money everywhere they could and did not know how to hold out longer, I must return at once. I finished my trip and took the next steamer home.

The company officers were all on the dock to greet me, and they might have looked more doleful, but I cannot imagine how. We went uptown, had luncheon, and they told me the worst. They owed $43,000,000, and no bank would lend a penny more, the factory was running but there were no sales, the commercial paper was falling due and they had no money to take it up with, and the contract materials were coming in and they could not pay for them. As a last resort, they had pledged the rubber on what are known as "certificates of importation." The case, as they put it, seemed hopeless. They were hopeless.

We reached Akron the next morning. It was a Friday morning. Things looked very blue at the office. Having looked about, I said:

"I will not tackle this job until Monday."

I went down to the Old Homestead to be alone and to think, and by Saturday I had finished my thinking. I telephoned the assistant sales manager to have three or four representative district sales managers, branch managers, and salesmen in my office Monday morning. I wanted to get a first-hand picture of what was going on in the field, for certainly we could not do business without sales.

On Monday morning we had our meeting. All the men there had about the same reasons to give me, which amounted to this:

"There is no business, the dealers are not only stocked but also demoralized and will not buy."

We talked a while, and then I went to the sales manager and said:

"I am going to be sales manager for thirty or sixty days. It may be a little embarrassing for you to be in this department without authority, and I think you had better take a vacation."

I had made up my mind exactly what I was going to do. Ours was not an impossible situation. Situations are only as impossible as one makes them. The sales organization had not been working for a long time. Orders had been handed to them, and they had gotten so soft that now, when real action was needed, they did not have it in them to take action.

They saw only closed doors everywhere and had not the nerve to open them.

The situation did not frighten me. It put new life into me. I saw the opportunity to do more business than we had ever done, but first the inertia of the sales force had to be overcome.

I wired for all the branch and district managers to come in. They were a cheerless-looking lot. What I said to them boils down to about this:

"We are in the business of making and selling tires. The factory here is piled to the roof with unsold tires. All the branches are full of tires. And so are all your dealers. The public has not stopped using tires, but they are not going to buy at present prices. Our tires have to be turned into cash. There is only one way to do that, and that is, to make such a big cut in prices that those tires will just have to sell.

"Therefore, we are reducing all our prices 25 percent It is up to you men to show the dealers that it is better business to move their stocks than to hang on to them. "We have plenty of tires to sell them, and they will make more money by getting rid of their stocks at a loss and restocking at the new price than they will by holding on to the tires they have in the hope of getting clear on them."

Many, I might almost say most, of the men could not understand such a price cut. They saw in it only a lot of trouble with the dealers, for with this one move we were cutting a quarter off the inventory of every dealer, and of course that meant trouble. All of the other tire companies were maintaining prices.

After I had made my announcement, the argument started. Some of the men thought that a 10 percent cut would be enough; others thought that we might go as high as 15 percent, but only a few could envision the effects of 25 percent. I did not tell them that I had been considering 33 1/3 percent. But I did tell them that a small reduction would not give the smash we had to have—the big dramatic play. For not otherwise could we attract the buying public.

These managers had to be convinced, for they had to carry the message out to the country—they had to have the enthusiasm I had for better business. Some would not be convinced and had to be let out. It was no time for half-hearted work.

We went to the country with a bang. For that was the way the thing had to go if it were to go at all. We had dealers' meetings all over the country. I went out on the road myself and addressed meetings. Any man who not willing to give up day and night to putting the sale over just had to get out. We spent money regardless in full-page advertisements in the newspapers. We hung big red banners on our dealers' shops, we hung them everywhere, and they had on them our slogan in red:

FIRESTONE TIRES 25 PERCENT DISCOUNT

It was a fire sale—for the first time in our history. We thrust aside all our dignity and customs. We plastered the country with our slogan.

Our competitors fought us for about a month—as I thought they would. Then they trailed after us with cuts. But I only needed that month's start.

That start gave us the business. In the months of September and October, 1920, we sold $18,000,000 worth of tires. That carried us out of the woods. We took up all the certificates of importation on rubber and reduced our borrowed money account from nearly forty-four millions to just over thirty-one millions.

Reducing the sales prices was only a small part of the work of getting back to normal. I have already described how we cut our office and sales forces. We also reduced our factory force in almost the same proportion, especially the non-productive labour.

But we were not entirely out of the financial woods. Our profits for 1921 were less than a million dollars. During the depth of the depression, it was necessary for the banks to carry the big companies in order to preserve a measure of stability.

On the thirty-first day of October, 1924, we did not owe a dollar to any bank!

By hammering on economies, by pressing sales and qualities, and by never fooling ourselves as to where we stood, we had wiped out an indebtedness which at one time was thought to be crushing.

It was not an easy road we travelled, but we safely got to the end.

212 " But why have we waited so long to attack the problem of having our own rubber sources? "

Chapter XVII
America Should Produce its Own Rubber

When the war broke out, the United States was building two great industries. When the war was over, we had built them. Since then, we have continued building those industries at a faster rate than any industries have ever been built.

I mean the automobile industry and the tire making industry. An automobile without a tire is useless; and so is a tire without an automobile. And yet these two great industries depend absolutely upon the will of foreign countries for their lives. They depend on rubber, and no rubber is grown in the United States.

We should be much more helpless without rubber than without leather. We have fairly good substitutes for leather—we can make almost first-class shoes without leather. It would be inconvenient to carry on without leather, but without rubber we could not carry on at all, for although we have rubber substitutes, none of them is practical when it comes to our big, important, essential use of rubber—automobile tires.

During the war, Germany had her most skilled chemists working on rubber substitutes, Probably, at this minute, many chemists are trying to discover how to make a commercial synthetic rubber. But as yet, no one has found an artificial rubber suitable for tires, nor has any one found a substitute for the rubber pneumatic or cushion tire.

The passenger car and the truck have changed the foundations of every sort of business in this country. Take away from us the motor vehicle, and I do not know what would happen. The damage would be more serious and lasting than if our land were laid waste by an invader. We could recover from the blowing up of New York City and all the big cities on the Atlantic seaboard more quickly than we could recover from the loss of our rubber. That is how important rubber is to us.

It is not so important to any other nation, for the life of no other nation is so dependent on the automobile as is ours. We have 85 percent of the world's automobiles. We use three quarters of the rubber production of the world, and of what we use, about 80 percent goes into automobile tires. And we grow only a very small fraction of 1 percent under our own flag! During the war we could not get a pound of rubber except upon the written consent of the British Government. I was then President of the Rubber Association of America and charged with the allotting of the rubber we were permitted to import. I have no complaint to make of the manner in which the British allowed us rubber, but the point is that we had to be allowed to bring in rubber. We were not then and are not now the masters of the rubber we use.

Great Britain controls more than 77 percent of the world's output; her rubber growers have put into effect a scheme for restricting production and exportation under Imperial auspices. This control of production may easily be translated into control of price. A rise of one cent per pound in the price of crude rubber, at our present consumption, costs the American owners between eight and nine million dollars annually. In 1922, we paid as little as 15 cents per pound. In 1925, we paid as high as $1.23. What is more, we are threatened with an actual shortage of rubber. We should have run into that shortage long since, had it not been that we have learned to make tires with four times the mileage of the tires of ten years ago, and are thus using less rubber per car mile. But with our tremendous automobile production, which is putting motor cars into every part of the globe, our demand for rubber will exceed the supply unless more rubber is planted.

I saw that some years back, but I could get no support. Three years ago it seemed imperative to go ahead with or without support. Congress made an appropriation of $500,000 to investigate sources of supply, and I also began an investigation of my own, sending experienced men through the world. American oil men have been prospecting and operating in foreign lands for years, but the rubber industry has been backward in caring for its own needs. I have already leased a million acres and started a large development in Liberia on the West Coast of Africa, which, if fully developed, will give us 200,000 tons a year, or about one half of America's present requirements, and insure the needs of our transportation. I am also investigating in the Philippines and other countries in the Far East. The government is experimenting in Florida. In a comparatively few years, I hope America will have an adequate supply of rubber.

But why have we waited so long to attack the problem of having our own rubber sources? Is there any mystery about growing rubber? Can it be had only from the Far East—like pearls?

Just why America has waited so long to control its own rubber supplies is a long story. Twenty-five years ago, the automobile was not important, and few even dreamed of the present industry. Some rubber came to us from Africa, but South America was the largest source. The jungles of Brazil are filled with wild rubber trees. These were tapped by the natives and eventually the crude rubber reached the trading posts on the Amazon and came into the hands of the white men. The cost of production was whatever the traders could induce the Indians to take for their rubber. We, in the business of making rubber goods, bought our rubber from the importers and had to take it according to the market price, and more or less regardless of quality. Most of us regarded rubber as a product of the jungles, and not as something which might be cultivated. Our requirements, in any event, were not large enough to make it worth while to look into sources of supply.

215

Brazil was glad enough to sell its rubber. In 1900, the world's production was less than fifty-four thousand tons, and of this only four tons was plantation—that is, cultivated—rubber from the Far East. The British and the Dutch, being always on the lookout for chances to invest abroad, saw the advantage of planting and cultivating rubber trees where they were more accessible and labour more plentiful, and they are to be given great credit for their vision. By 1907, the British and the Dutch had half a million acres in rubber plantations in Ceylon, the Federated Malay States, the Straits Settlements, and the Dutch East Indies.

The Brazilian politicians, in the meantime, thinking they had a stranglehold on the rubber, saw a source of revenue and clapped on an exorbitant export tax. In 1910, rubber brought as high as three dollars a pound, and the profits of the Brazilian traders and the government were enormous. But so also were the profits of the Far East plantations which had reached production. One company paid a dividend of 375 percent! That started the British plantation rubber boom. Brazil's tax was killing its rubber export, but the politicians could not see that. They held to their tax, and by 1914, the plantation rubber production exceeded that of wild rubber. The British and the Dutch cultivated their rubber to a point where its quality was fairly even, and they imposed standards of cleanliness which make it cheaper for the manufacturer to work with plantation than with wild rubber.

And so Brazil's output is only one half of what it was twenty-five years ago, and now it is hardly more than 5 percent of the world's production. Brazil let a great industry slip away while the British and Dutch were putting some four million acres and more than half a billion dollars into rubber. Until 1919, these companies boomed and their shares were leaders on the London Stock Exchange. A list of eleven of the large companies shows average annual cash dividends over nine years of about 100 percent. The companies put some of their profits into new planting but very little into surplus. Then came the business smash of 1920, and American tire makers found themselves with warehouses full of rubber, bought at more than fifty cents a pound, and rubber selling in the open market at fifteen cents. In 1921, rubber reached a high of twenty-one cents and a low of twelve cents, while in the next year the high was twenty-nine cents and the low fourteen cents. The rubber growers asked for government aid—they had spent all their money in dividends and had no surplus to tide them over. The British growers confused underconsumption with overproduction. They were advised to restrict production. They tried to restrict by agreement, but it did not work. The British Colonial office placed a restriction on rubber known as the Stevenson Restriction Act, which has been the cause of much trouble.

This Act takes the output of 1920 as normal and restricts exportation to 60 percent of that normal; each grower has his allotment, and if he exports over his quota, he pays a sliding scale tax, not merely on the excess, but upon his whole export. The law went into effect in November, 1922, and in a short time the price of rubber rose from fourteen cents to thirty-seven cents a pound and was even forced above a dollar. The technical features of the Act are too complicated to give here, but the real purpose under the familiar guise of "stabilizing" the price is to enrich a small group of rubber company shareholders and also to help out British finances by taking advantage of the fact that England has a rubber monopoly. Winston Churchill made the statement: "One of the principal means of paying the debt to America is in the provision of rubber." I decided to conduct an investigation into rubber on my own account, because, if our business were to perform a public service, it was our duty to keep open the way to the sources of raw material. We could not rely solely on government investigations. So in May, 1923, I cabled our Singapore manager, who has had twenty years' experience in the rubber-growing industry in the Far East, to employ a staff of two or three of the best planting experts. They proceeded at once to the Philippine Islands for a survey. They spent several weeks on the main island making inquiry into governmental conditions, and also visited the islands of Mindanao and Basilan, where several experiments in plantation rubber production had been made.

217

Upon their return they reported that the soil and climatic conditions in the southern islands of Philippine group were in every way equal to the conditions in any other rubber-producing country of the East, and that it was their opinion that rubber could be planted as economically as in any part of the British rubberproducing colonies or in the Dutch East Indies. They also felt that the labour problem was possible of solution. Because of the land laws now in force in the Philippines and the attitude of the native government, our investigators advised against then attempting any large rubber developments in the Philippines. If the Philippines are to be developed, capital must have assurance that it will be properly protected, which the present political situation does not assure.

Following the return of the Philippine investigation party, I sent two of its members into Mexico. They examined several plantation properties in southern Mexico, but before they could complete their investigation, a revolution broke out and they were forced to leave the country by way of Guatemala. They continued their investigation of the possibilities of rubber production through Central America, including Panama. They found climatic and soil conditions suitable, plenty of land, but no adequate supply of labour.

In December, 1923, my attention was called to the country of Liberia on the West Coast of Africa. I sent a representative to Liberia, where he found a 2,000-acre plantation planted in 1910 with Hevea trees, which are the standard and best producing species and used throughout the East. This plantation had been abandoned shortly after the war began, and its lease reverted to the Liberian Government. Although it had received no attention for several years, our representative tapped the trees and found the flow of the latex equal to or better than that of the Far East. He returned to America at once and reported that climate, soil, and labour conditions in Liberia were equal to, if not better than, those in any part of the Eastern rubber-producing areas where he had spent seventeen years in rubber cultivation.

In April, 1924, he, accompanied by two experienced rubber planters and two other men who had spent several years on the West Coast of Africa and Liberia, returned to Liberia to make a thorough survey. They explored hundreds of miles into the interior to determine the topography and suitability of the country for rubber growing and also to find out about the availability and condition of the labour. It is estimated that there are 2,000,000 natives in Liberia. They found the native population to be of a healthy and vigorous type and apparently willing workers. He took over the 2,000-acre plantation, cleared the undergrowth, and began tapping. In a few months, he had confirmed our preliminary reports as to the possibilities of the economical production of rubber. We also did some preliminary work in clearing the jungle in order to determine the character of the labour and the actual cost of planting.

With this expedition I also sent a representative to Liberia to confer with the Liberian Government as to an agreement to take over lands for rubber planting on a large scale. The outcome of that agreement I have already referred to.

In September, 1925, we leased a 35,000-acre plantation in the State of Chiapas, Mexico, that has 350 acres in Hevea rubber trees and several thousand more in Castilloa. Our investigators had been on this plantation in 1923 when they were driven out by a revolution. We sent an experienced planter there in October, 1925. He found all buildings destroyed by fire and the improvements in a deplorable condition. It is difficult to get labour there, and there is great uncertainty in governmental affairs, the property being liable to raid at any time. Therefore, it may be impossible for us to make much of a development in Mexico. We found that soil, climatic, and health conditions are suitable.

All of the above have been personal efforts. But the largest personal effort is not enough in so serious a situation as rubber. Before the Committee of Interstate and Foreign Commerce of the House of Representatives, I said, in part, on January 15, 1926:

"It is my opinion that if America is to attain any degree of independence in its source of supply of rubber as well as other materials, which are now in the hands of foreign monopoly, our government must give proper encouragement to capital and must assure the industries interested that it will lend its utmost assistance in protecting our investments. This particularly applies to rubber, for it is necessary to make a large capital investment.

"I recognize the difficulties involved in this suggestion. I do not presume to speak with reference to our foreign policy. Surely, however, it is practicable to recommend that our government take active steps to remove those laws in the Philippine Islands which are an effective barrier against large-scale development of rubber plantations there and to enact such laws as would encourage the investment of capital in the Philippine Islands. An awakened public sense of the dangers which threaten our sources of supply may be regarded as of the highest importance.

I do not favour a subsidy in the form of an import tax or in any other form whatsoever, nor do I favour any measures which may be regarded as in any sense retaliatory toward the British Government or any other foreign country.

"The proper solution of the problem in my opinion is the investment of American capital on a large scale in plantations for rubber production. These investments must largely be made in foreign countries, at great distances and in large amounts.

It is an industry of large figures. This is illustrated by the fact that latest figures available indicate the investment by British investors of the huge sum of $500,000,000 in the rubber-producing industry. The American people will make the necessary investments of their capital in these far-off countries only if they feel assured of the sympathetic support of their own government, and in my opinion our government should do everything within its power, consistent with its foreign policies, to encourage such investments."

What I said before the Congressional Committee applies particularly to Liberia and the Philippines. We have been offered concessions in the Philippines which we may or may not take up—according to the assurance that the terms will be carried out.

Liberia is a child of the United States—it is the result of a philanthropic movement in this country, begun more than a hundred years ago, to return the Negro slaves to their African homeland. The territory was bought with American money, the government was set up with American money, and on the American model. In an official communication to President Roosevelt in 1909 Secretary of State Elihu Root stated: "Liberia is an American colony…It is unnecessary to argue that the duty of the United States toward the unfortunate victims of the slave trade was not completely performed in landing them upon the coast of Africa, and that our nation rests under the highest obligation to assist them, so far as they need assistance, toward the maintenance of free, orderly, and prosperous civil society. The interest of the people of the United States in the welfare and progress of the millions of American citizens of the black race in the United States also furnishes strong reasons for helping to maintain this colony, whose success in self-government will give hope and courage, and whose failure would bring discouragement to the entire race."

This communication was in connection with an investigation into the condition of Liberia by an official government commission, which inquiry had been requested by the Liberians in an application to the United States for aid in maintaining its independence and political integrity, and the loan of assistance in administering its financial and governmental affairs. This plea was the outgrowth of continual disputes with the colonial governments of their neighbours, Great Britain and France, who the American Commission found had been constantly encroaching upon Liberian territory.

The Commission recommended that the United States officially assist Liberia in maintaining its boundaries, reorganizing its finances, and developing its hinterland. It was cordially supported by the State Department and President Taft, who wrote Congress: "I trust that the policy of the United States toward Liberia will be so shaped as to fulfil our national duty to the Liberian people, who by the efforts of this Government and through the material support of American citizens, were established on the African coast and set on the pathway to sovereign statehood."

In commenting upon the Liberian people, the American Commission said it was "impressed with the dignity and intelligence of the representatives of the government with whom it had dealings...The Liberians are not a revolutionary people. Since the beginning of their national life, they have maintained the forms of orderly government...Despite frequent assertions to the contrary, Liberia is not bankrupt...In contrast to the natural wealth of the country, it (national debt of $1,300,000 in 1909) is very small."

The Commission points out that the maintenance of its borders, chiefly as a result of the partition of African by European powers, has kept Liberia occupied politically to the detriment of its commercial and industrial development. To the west Liberia has the British colony of Sierra Leone, also established as a colony for freed black men. On the north and east are the French colonies of Guinea and the Ivory Coast.

The 43,000 square miles composing Liberia lie well within the world's rubber belt, extending from four to eight degrees north of the Equator. It is bounded for 350 miles on the south by the Atlantic Ocean and is within 4,000 miles of New York by direct steamer route. There is an average at present of more than one steamer a day calling at Monrovia (named after President Monroe), the capital and principal port, and it is a port of regular call for two steamship lines to America and six to Europe and England. It has numerous rivers navigable for from twenty-five to ninety-five miles from the sea. Its land transportation, however, is totally undeveloped, there being no railroads and only a few miles of passable roadways. Road building, harbour improvement, and installation of lines of communication are included in my plan.

The land for the most part is well drained, much of it consisting of gently sloping hills with intervening wide, winding depressions. Forests cover almost the entire area, but there is comparatively a small amount of "big bush" or virgin jungle. This is due, for the most part, to the rotating system of cultivation practised by the natives for centuries. Each family clears and plants a new area each year, refusing to use the same cleared land until seven years or more have elapsed. This system has not robbed the soil of its fertility, and at the same time has made the work of clearing for rubber plantations less expensive because secondarygrowth timber is much easier to remove than virgin jungle.

Health conditions in Liberia are exceptional for the tropics. The natives are strong and healthy. Their villages and huts are clean and as sanitary as is possible under primitive conditions. It is not uncommon for a native carrier or porter to travel thirty miles in ten hours with a burden of forty to sixty pounds balanced on his head. Among 500 natives employed upon our 2,000-acre plantation, fifteen miles inland, there was only one case of illness during the last year. This is a remarkable record, for it is not uncommon among the plantation operations of the Far East to have 30 percent of the labour force absent at one time on account of illness. Sleeping sickness, yellow fever, and other plagues are rare in Liberia, although quite prevalent at other places on the West Coast of Africa.

Under the terms of an agreement entered into with the government of the Republic of Liberia, I have been granted a lease for ninety-nine years on 1,000,000 acres of land most suitable for the production of crude rubber; another lease for a like period upon the plantation of 2,000 acres which was planted fifteen years ago and is in full bearing; and an arrangement for the general public improvement of the country, such as the construction of port and harbor facilities, roads, hospitals, sanitation, lines of communication, and the development of hydro-electric power.

The cost of reclaiming the jungle and bringing rubber into bearing in Liberia will be a minimum of $100 per acre, or a total of $100,000,000 to develop the full acreage of our lease. To operate such a development at capacity will require the employment of 350,000 native labourers. For the last year our factories have been receiving shipments of highest grade rubber from this plantation. Clearing operations were begun upon thousands of acres of land several months ago. A large labour force has already been organized, and a staff of expert planters and their assistants are already on the ground.

223

The operating plan for the first year calls for an organization consisting of a medical staff, sanitary engineer, mechanical engineer, architect and builder, soil expert, forester, and their staffs, as well as twenty planting units each in charge of an expert planter and his assistants. These men will recruit and organize the thousands of native labourers required.

I believe that we can build up Liberia through our own operations to a point where, in addition to being our great rubber source, it will also be a large market for American goods. This will be serving the people in a practical way.

224 "Business is made up of opportunities for great sacrifices and great accomplishments"

Chapter XVIII
Why I am in Business

There is a notion that if a man has established a business and accumulated a certain competence and then keeps on working, it is only because he is greedy and wants more and more money and that eventually he becomes just a slave—a slave to money.

Nothing could be further from the facts. It is true that for twenty-five years I have been building a business. I have given it all of my time and thought. I am still giving it all of my time and thought and intend to keep on doing so.

I do not know whether I am the slave or the master of that business. But the big thing is that I do not care which, for the job is worth doing as either master or servant. The job is not only worth doing well, but there is a great joy in doing it.

All other considerations aside, the very worries and insistent demands on one's mentality and physique are a joy—for they are tests, challenges.

Business is not a game. Business is not a science—there are too many unknown and unknowable factors ever to permit it to be a science. If business were a science, then one could learn the principles and let the thing run itself. But no business will run itself. Perhaps business is a profession—of that I am not sure. But rather I think that business comprehends everything, and that is one of the reasons why I like to be in it.

The money side is not unimportant. It is very important. Naturally, one needs quite a lot of money in order to live, but the bulk of what I earn goes back into the company. I am willing to stand or fall by the business. That business must earn money, and therefore it has to be watched day and night. It must earn money, else it will fail, and failure means that one has played the game and lost.

Deliberately causing a business to operate without profits through some foggy concept of benevolence is only another way of destroying the service of that business. For unless a business earns, it must stop. The game has to be played or not played. There is no point in between.

And so I stay in business and I take on additional burdens, and I intend to keep on taking on additional burdens for these reasons: Our life is made up of experiences. Business leads one into every profession and every walk of life. It is the school of experience.

The greatest pleasure is in doing something to help others to help themselves. There is some small satisfaction in just giving away money, but the great satisfaction is in giving others the chance to be independent. For instance, the opening of Liberia or the Philippines would be worth more than a life's work. I like people, and business brings one in close contact with a never-ending stream of people.

And, finally, there is the supreme satisfaction of accomplishment—of planning to do something and of carrying through those plans against all obstacles to a final accomplishment.

Business is made up of opportunities for great sacrifices and great accomplishments.

It is the most absorbing occupation on earth.

The End

fs

CPSIA information can be obtained
at www.ICGtesting.com
Printed in the USA
LVHW072041190723
752585LV00086B/1055/J